THE HUMAN IMPACT OF HYPERMARKETS AND SUPERSTORES

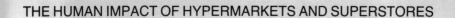

To Alice and George

The Human Impact of Hypermarkets and Superstores

A. G. HALLSWORTH
Department of Geography
Portsmouth Polytechnic

Avebury

Aldershot · Brookfield USA · Hong Kong · Singapore · Sydney

Published by

Avebury

Gower Publishing Company Limited,
Gower House, Croft Road, Aldershot,
Hants. GU11 3HR, England.

Gower Publishing Company,
Old Post Road, Brookfield, Vermont 05036
USA.

British Library Cataloguing in Publication Data
Hallsworth, Alan G., 1947-
    The human impact of hypermarkets and
    superstores
    1. Great Britain. Hypermarkets & Superstores
    I. Title
    381'.1

ISBN 0 566 05733 6

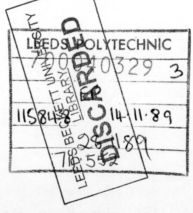

Printed and bound in Great Britain by
Athenaeum Press Limited, Newcastle upon Tyne

Contents

Figures

Tables

Acknowledgements

I am indebted to Rob Potter, Mike Bateman and the many planners and retailers who helped bring about the successful completion of the original research on which this study is based.

Carol, Jim, Roger and Sundra of the Geography Department, Portsmouth Polytechnic all made substantial contributions to the final format of the work.

Dr Mayer Hillman of Policy Studies Institute, London NW1 kindly gave permission for the reproduction of table 2.1.

Responsibility for any errors rests solely with myself.

1 Introduction: aims of study and the study area

One of the most distinctive trends in retailing in post-war Britain has been the decline in the total number of retail outlets, accompanied by a rise in the average size of each outlet. In the food retailing sector new types of store format have emerged in the last 20 years. The superstore, a large in-centre or edge-of-centre outlet, made its appearance in the 1960s and, in 1972, Carrefour - Europe's largest retail organisation - introduced the bigger, out-of-town, French style hypermarket. Such a massive restructuring carries with it the implication that new formats may leave certain areas less well served than previously and it may be that one of the two major new store formats is to be preferred on welfare grounds. Some have made the point that the remoteness of the hypermarket must inevitably mean that it discriminates against the less mobile consumer who is probably also disadvantaged in other ways. Intuitively one is inclined to accept the logic of this argument though it is an argument that has rarely been investigated empirically.

This study seeks to fill this gap in the cumulated knowledge of the trading effects of hypermarkets and superstores by means of a direct comparison of the two types of outlet. The assumption that the locational characteristics of hypermarkets and superstores have inherently different implications for the social welfare of consumers is directly addressed. It follows that the results will have implications for the role of the planning profession in seeking socially-equitable outcomes. This is especially topical given the current pressures upon planners to adopt more *laissez-faire* attitudes to retail competition and the fears expressed in some quarters that market forces are not the proper mechanism for regulating spatial outcomes.

Confidence that this study may well shed light on issues of national concern must be tempered by the realisation that retailing does not operate in a vacuum. The retail trade is subject to the same complex forces as those affecting other sectors of the economy - with the additional difficulty of the necessity to make allowance for the frictional effects of distance when trading performance is compared. Initially it is useful to assess some of the major problems that may be anticipated when issues of social welfare are clarified by reference to actual store trading characteristics. One possibility would be that welfare problems could be illustrated by the discovery of circumstances of absolute disadvantage where an area loses totally what was once a satisfactory level of retail provision; probably as a result of store closure. In fact, after many years of retail analysis, very few instances have ever been found where store closures could be attributed unequivocally to the advent of a major new hypermarket or superstore in the immediate vicinity. Furthermore, the barriers to entry to the retail trade are so low that few major urban areas in this country would ever be likely to suffer total loss of trade. Far more likely is the possibility of finding instances of relative disadvantage where the best and newest retail opportunities are located in such a way that they are not an effective shopping opportunity for certain groups in certain areas.

Relative disadvantage is a distinct possibility when the retail trade is evolving new store formats that are larger but more spatially dispersed. Current work on polarisation theory suggests that the development of hypermarkets and superstores has tended to have greatest market impact on high street supermarkets which have become less cost-effective and are being shunned by some of the major retail chains. It is suggested that supermarkets are closed for policy reasons that favour superstores and hypermarkets. The total market polarises between these new large stores and a revitalised small store sector that thrives in the interstices between the large stores. Some communities may find that they have lost the provision of a high street supermarket but gained a larger store nearby and much improved small local outlets. For many, the addition of the superstore or hypermarket will be advantageous but should that store be too far away for everyone to

reach easily then some will clearly be disadvantaged by the
market changes. At a more subtle level, certain communities
will suffer relative disadvantage if the retail provision in
their area does not change at all but other areas receive new
store formats that offer their residents more attractive
shopping.

Reference has been made only to the food retailing sector,
yet non-food retailing too has been drastically altered, for
example, by the introduction of DIY 'sheds' and by proposals
for out-of-town malls. The argument in this study is that
welfare problems are best brought out through reference to
basic staples of everyday life: food requirements, rather than
by any differences observable in the provision of non-essen-
tials or luxury goods. Indeed, it seems unlikely that one
could quantify and compare the advantage accruing to a high-
income area that had just received a new DIY outlet as opposed
to a low-income area that had received a new carpet warehouse.
A very great deal of the definition of what is 'best' or
'preferred' is to be found only in the mind of the consumer in
her, or his, local milieu. The desire here is to base much of
the investigation of welfare upon the perceptions of individuals. This points to yet another advantage of comparing
hypermarkets and superstores. They are large outlets which
rapidly become familiar landmarks in their local area; they
are 'imageable' in the minds of a large percentage of the
population in a way that small stores cannot be. This advantage is compounded by the fact that they sell in bulk the
types of items - dry groceries, meat, greengrocery, dairy
products and so on - that all households need regularly.
Because demand for such goods is regular and relatively
inelastic, food shopping is inescapable and most individuals are soon aware of changes to the local food retailing
provision. A perceptual analysis of foodstores is far more
likely to succeed than a perceptual analysis of store types
that are only used by certain segments of the population.

The type of study area required for this work was determined
by the nature of the problem under investigation. An area had
to be found where all the wider trends of post-war retail
change had been experienced and where all types of food outlet
would be present. The major necessity was for an archetypal
superstore, demonstrating the characteristics of in-centre or
edge-of-centre location, that could readily be compared with a
genuinely out-of-town hypermarket. The difference had to be
one not merely of size but also of location, with one store
being markedly more accessible to the 'normal' flow of shopper
traffic into an established retail centre. The fact that
there are far fewer hypermarkets than superstores reduced the

3

range of possible study sites which was reduced still further
by the stringent requirement that the stores be imageable in
order to assist a perceptual analysis. Retail styles change
rapidly and store layout and design soon becomes dated, making
it unrealistic to attempt to compare a new store with one just
a few years old. Differences in design would, in such circumstances, be compounded by the fact that an older store would
have established a firm trading base and local clientele.

THE STUDY AREA
The chosen study region is best seen within the broad context
of South East Hampshire (Figure 1.1) since this is the overall
Structure Planning sub-division. The 1970s, leading up to the
construction of the two stores, were broadly a period of growth
for South Hampshire. Throughout the period an average of 5,000
new houses a year were constructed; in line with the expected
rate of new household formation and despite the economic
downturn that accompanied the election of the Thatcher government in 1979. From 1971 to 1981 the region was able to show a
modest net increase in the total numbers of jobs, though this
masks major structural changes in the types of jobs held.
Growth was especially strong in the tertiary and quaternary
sectors whilst the secondary manufacturing sector, as elsewhere, experienced losses. The area is still targeted for
economic growth despite poor performance in the national
economy, with the result that population is predicted to rise
from 900,000 in 1981 to between 1,020,000 and 1,070,000 in
1996 (Hampshire County Council, 1978).

As will be seen later when the planning of the county is
studied in detail, the underlying trend of the post-war period
has been one of growth, and this is especially the case with
the period from the late 1960s onwards. The area chosen for
study was the Portsmouth, Southampton city, region, containing
two of the largest cities in the South East and with all the
customary problems and demands of major city, regions. The
area had several designated growth zones, though most of these
were in the Southampton area. Growth in the Portsmouth area
had been more 'organic' particularly since 1976 when a planned
growth sector west of Waterlooville was deleted from the structure plan. The area had seen substantial motorway development
with the M27 linking the two major cities, the M275 feeding
into Portsmouth's rapidly developing Continental Ferry Port
and the A3(M) looping northwards from Portsmouth towards London.
Regionally, much emphasis needs to be placed upon the levels
of car ownership since both the stores under study are geared
primarily to the car-owning sectors of the population. Disaggregation of car ownership figures to the level of the Enumeration District (ED) will be a feature of the empirical

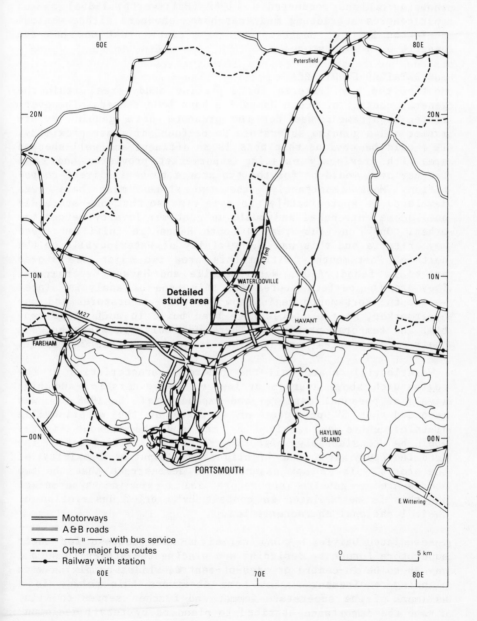

Figure 1.1 The general study region (detailed study area outlined).

analysis and dramatic differences will emerge. At the regional
level, though, the picture is very healthy and an analysis of
shopping centres conducted in 1969 (Hallsworth, 1985c) showed
most centres attracting many car-borne shoppers with a maximum
at Totton West of Southampton - a centre that now has the
benefit of a superstore.

THE DETAILED STUDY AREA

Most of the key criteria for a precise study area within the
general context of South Hampshire have been stated. The over-
riding requirement was for the presence of a genuine hypermarket and a genuine superstore to be found in close proximity.
It should be obvious that this is an affluent and well-shopped
area with previously existing supermarket provision and so a
further need would be for the two stores to be in direct competition. Most importantly, the two stores must have been
developed at approximately the same time so that one store did
not become entrenched and build up customer loyalty before the
other. Only one sub-area in south Hampshire fulfilled these
key criteria and this was the vicinity of Waterlooville to the
north of Portsmouth. Within this area two major new stores
are to be found; ASDA, Waterlooville and Havant Hypermarket.
They are the perfect stores for this type of analysis since,
whilst the Portsmouth region now has nine superstores and one
hypermarket, no two stores have been built in such close spatial and temporal proximity. There was only six weeks between
their opening dates, and they are located less than 3km apart.

Waterlooville shares all the general characteristics of the
region with above average affluence, car ownership, and high
levels of personal earnings and expenditure. In 1969, it was
recorded that 59 per cent of shoppers at the Waterlooville
district centre had arrived by car and the present figures
would be considerably higher. Figure 1.2 illustrates the
detailed study area and highlights the spatial proximity of
the stores. It is now essential to demonstrate that the two
stores are a genuine superstore and a genuine hypermarket
and this is best placed in context by a brief description of
their locational characteristics.

Associated Dairies (ASDA) gained notable success for their
superstore format by designing and placing the stores in such a
way as to be in-centre or edge-of-centre, whilst complying with
planning requirements. For some observers this policy is a
hallmark of the superstore format and further serves to illustrate the importance ascribed to planners by retail decision-
makers. Certainly planning opposition to the out-of-town
hypermarket has been a feature of post-war planning.

6

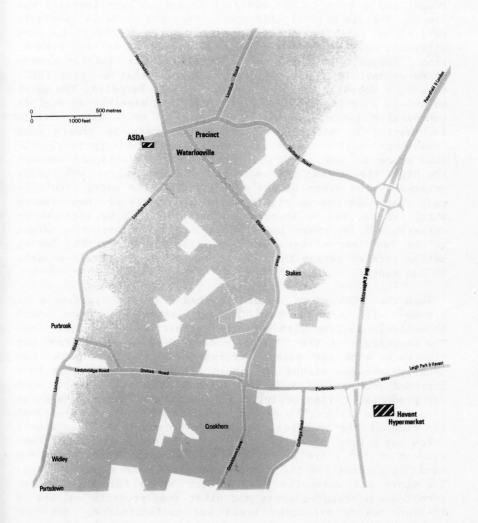

Figure 1.2 The detailed study area, including ASDA,
Waterlooville and Havant Hypermarket.

ASDA WATERLOOVILLE

In the 1970s, ASDA embarked upon a planned expansion from their base in the north of England into the south. They developed a superstore of approximately 5,000m^2 in Gosport, which lies within the general study area, and this opened for trading in 1977. Further possible superstore sites within the area were sought and a site in the District Centre at Waterlooville was found. What is most significant is that the store is genuinely part of an existing shopping centre and locationally no more difficult to reach than the supermarkets of an earlier generation. Indeed, at the time of opening, the District Centre at Waterlooville had three major supermarkets: a Tesco (PLC) outlet, a Cooperative store and a Shoppers Paradise. The major advantage accruing to ASDA was that it had directly accessible car parking spaces which the others did not. Waterlooville is bisected by both the A3 and B2150 roads to create four 'quadrants' each of which has some associated car parking. The ASDA store in the south-west quadrant was positioned between the High Street and the 600 car parking spaces eventually created by the sweep of the relief road. The point should be made that ASDA has no rights of exclusive use of these spaces which can be used by shoppers to other stores, by local shop-workers, and by other local people. The south-west quadrant is the best served for car parking resulting in ASDA having better parking access than any of the other 150 retail outlets in the centre.

When the ASDA store opened it had a gross floorspace of 5,956m^2 with approximately 3,523m^2 sales floorspace which is entirely in line with standard definitions of a superstore. The percentage of the floorspace devoted to non-food items has fluctuated with the sales performance of such goods but has usually averaged around 50 percent. The non-food sales have included such items as TV and electrical goods, toys, paint, car products, garden products and clothing. There is also an area for the sale of books, newspapers and magazines and, at the time of the empirical research, the store had a cafeteria which has since been removed. By far the most significant element of the store is its food sales areas, since these are known to account for the bulk of purchases made at superstores. The store has extensive refrigerator space for the sale of uncooked and prepared meats and other food products and has an in-store bakery producing bread and confectionery. Substantial amounts of floorspace are devoted to packaged and canned goods, which have usually been dominated by branded goods sold at highly competitive prices. There is a cheese and delicatessen area and an off-licence and soft drinks section. The store has never offered a fresh fish sales area though vacuum-packed chilled fish products were later introduced.

The store emerges as a typical modern superstore offering a wide range of food and non-food products in an attractive environment. The external appearance of the store is enhanced by the usage of red brick facings and tiled roof. The sloping site necessitated the construction of an 'auto-walk' for the conveyance of shopping trolleys to the main car park at the rear of the store.

HAVANT HYPERMARKET
As with ASDA, Waterlooville, the present concern lies not with the convoluted planning history between 1977 and 1980 but with the characteristics of the store that came to be built. By far the most significant factor is the proximity of the store to a motorway interchange since only a bank of earth separates the store from the A3(M) motorway. The store does not feed directly onto the motorway system but onto the feeder road via a roundabout constructed at the expense of Portsea Island Mutual Co-operative Society (PIMCO). The second key point is that the store was constructed in isolation from other stores, commercial premises or other transport focii. This inevitably meant that the store was likely to fall foul of objections to out-of-town shopping. Havant Hypermarket is not in an established shopping location but on the extreme periphery of the built-up urban area and was always vulnerable to objections on environmental grounds. Most significantly, for the purposes of this study, it was in a location sufficiently remote that only the nearby residents of Leigh Park overspill housing estate could expect to reach it easily without a car.

With a gross floorspace of $10,684m^2$ and sales area of $6,503m^2$ the store is an archetypal hypermarket and one of the largest in southern England. It was eventually built on a 25.2 acre site and was provided with exclusive use of 1,200 car parking spaces split into three separate parking areas. In terms of providing retail facilities it is a larger version of ASDA, Waterlooville; for example, the restaurant was constructed to seat 168 persons in $929m^2$ of floorspace and there were 36 checkouts compared with ASDA's 26. That apart, the store replicates the pattern at ASDA, Waterlooville with an in-store bakery, even more extensive refrigerator space and a fuller range of non-food items.

The position is that the two stores cover the same general types of goods but that Havant Hypermarket has the wider selection and it also carries Co-operative brand products as its 'own label' goods. When the food sales areas are compared, Havant Hypermarket only differs markedly from ASDA, Waterlooville in the fact that it has a fishmonger among its specialist attractions. Beyond the checkouts, however, there is a wider range of concessions and these initially included a jewellers, newsagents and ice-cream specialist. This store is of a much simpler construction with the main building consisting of a simple steel frame erected on piled foundations with brick cladding to a height of 2.6 metres. Insulated metal cladding continues to a height of approximately 8 metres and the roof is metal decked and covers an area of 2.5 acres. It is clear that the materials and the method of construction were chosen to ensure completion of construction in the shortest possible time.

STORE LOCATIONS
Given the brief to find two stores that could be analysed in order to point out contrasts between an archetypal superstore and an archetypal hypermarket, ASDA, Waterlooville and Havant Hypermarket could hardly be more appropriate. As Figure 1.2 shows they are in very close proximity, being less than three kilometres apart, yet their locations contrast dramatically in character from in-centre to motorway, oriented. They are both large stores that will be 'imageable' by the local population, for whom they have become the largest food shopping stores. The requirement that one store should not be markedly older than the other is almost completely met since ASDA opened less than six weeks before Havant Hypermarket. This also means that they were developed under the same planning controls - both are in the Borough of Havant.

Issues of substantial signficance in terms of social welfare are to be addressed and an excellent study area has been iden-tified for this purpose. Should major differences between the two stores emerge then this has clear implications for the identification of preferred store types and this calls forth the need for mechanisms to ensure that the better types of store are built. Though the planning profession is currently under great pressure from 'free market' forces, the logical step would be to identify policies that maximise the likelihood of socially-equitable outcomes and this is an ultimate aim of the study. It has already been seen that it was impossible to place the two stores in context without reference to planners and planning. The historical development of the stores is intrinsically tied up with the planning philosophies prevailing at the time of their development. Even more significant than planning as an influence, however, are the wider forces in the economy that have brought about the development of hypermarkets and superstores and that ensure that there will be pressure for these types of stores into the foreseeable future. This study is not cast historically as a record of past events in a particular location, but rather looks forward to future growth in large stores when even more hypermarkets and super-stores will be in close competition.

The procedure will be to outline in Chapter two the nature of 'human impacts' or 'welfare' approaches and decision-making in their wider context. Chapter three will outline the chosen techniques with an emphasis upon the ways in which behavioural techniques have previously been used in retail analysis. The subsequent chapters deal with the empirical analysis of the two stores with a succession of approaches bringing out welfare themes, commencing in Chapter four with a study of shoppers at the two stores. Chapter five presents a perceptual analysis of the two stores in the belief that welfare is essentially subjective in nature, whilst Chapter six considers in more detail the welfare characteristics of the individuals who choose to shop at the two stores. The final chapter, seven, presents the policy prescriptions that flow from the empirical analysis.

It can therefore be seen that this study approaches the subject of superstores and hypermarkets by first setting them in a wider context. Aspects of welfare are then discussed and techniques are chosen that will highlight welfare issues. The empirical analysis is in three stages which are consecutive and cumulative. Results from one stage feed into the next in order to build up a picture of the welfare-related contrasts between two archetypal stores. Only when all this is completed are policy suggestions made.

2 Welfare, manageralism and retail change

INTRODUCTION

The proposal in this study is that planners are most likely to be the agents of socially just spatial outcomes and this requires ample justification. Massive retail change is taking place and any trends identified here will be magnified in the future. However, a necessary prelude to an examination of the role of planners as managers of the urban system was the identification of precisely how welfare and social justice can conceivably be measured.

It was therefore necessary to consider some of the approaches that had been adopted for the analysis of welfare problems whilst at the same time recognising that welfare approaches to retailing have seldom been attempted. One of the most common avenues of welfare study has been through Pareto-type analyses. Harvey (1973, p.55) outlines the Pareto-optimum situation as one in which nobody can become better off without making someone else worse off.

This might appear to be a fruitful approach since one could hopefully measure the extent to which a new store in a new location affected the shopping opportunities of residents in the catchment area. The major difficulty lies with the problem of establishing an equilibrium in shopping against which change might be measured. Pareto-type approaches have most commonly been used in the context of the housing market and even here situations of equilibrium are hard to find; such is the scale of change. From the preceding chapter it has been learned that the scale of change in the retail sector is rapid indeed and it is hard to conceive of a stable year from which to draw patterns of change - a problem compounded by woefully poor statistical information. It would require a most unusual combination of circumstances for any area to show total stability. It would probably require a static population, no store changes, no increases in personal affluence and no changes in mobility patterns. Such a situation is infinitely less likely than one where growth in all of those factors would lead to a new store being provided simply to cater for new demand.

Paretian approaches are entirely dependent on an equilibrium and there is probably already enough evidence that any approach that makes assumptions of being able to measure change by reference to such an equilibrium is not going to be at all helpful in the context of this work. Even in the area of housing studies where Pareto approaches are common, Harvey (1973, p.55) claims that:

"These models provide us with important insights
into the allocation mechanisms which underline
the formation of an urban structure, but they
tell us little about how a given distribution
.... comes about."

When Havant Hypermarket and ASDA Waterlooville are subsequently discussed in more detail it will become obvious that no assumptions about an equilibrium can apply in south-east Hampshire. Here the rate of retail change since the war has been spectacular, and this must surely destroy any hope of a Pareto-type approach. Though the requirement for growth and change is met, leading to the possibility of examining the 'new' situation, the scale of change is too fast. Noah (1973, p.65) is particularly dismissive of the Paretian approaches:

"Welfare economics, particularly in its present
Paretian form has become the last refuge of an
unrealistic general-equilibrium approach, and a
reverential attitude towards the market system."

It was clearly necessary to examine just how change is likely to occur in order to decide how best it might be analysed. It was initially felt unlikely that any area, certainly in south-east Hampshire, would be left totally unserved by retail provision and this seems to remove the possibility of identifying absolute disadvantage. Since this study concentrates on two stores in suburban southern England that are only some three kilometres apart, the likelihood of absolute disadvantage became even more improbable. Considerable attention had also to be paid to the major complications introduced by the notion that shopping has a social function, allowing people to meet others whilst on shopping trips away from the home. When the concept of retail image is added to this and the idea of preferred stores or store types is introduced, then even relative disadvantage is likely to be very difficult to assess. There is a phenomenological aspect to the study that cannot be ignored and it is even difficult to draw upon the existing literature on public service provision since a retail store cannot be compared with a fire station, though some might see both as 'impure public goods'. The latter is not subject to individual preferences and judgements and simply functions 'equally' for all consumers – a retail store clearly does not. Accordingly, one can conceive of a situation where a new store is added to an area, is too far for a certain set of consumers to reach, and does not affect existing retail provision in the vicinity of those consumers. Some of these distant consumers will feel no disadvantage from the changed situation whilst others will acutely regret the fact that they cannot reach what they perceived as an attractive new store. Such conceptualisations serve to confirm the importance of behaviour and perception as measures of relative disadvantage.

At the same time it has to be recognised that Paretian approaches are not the only welfare-based measures of relative disadvantage and Smith (1977) has outlined the attractions of the Lorenz curve. At its most simple level the Lorenz curve measures the equality of distributions and is not dependent upon stability, growth or decline of the patterns under scrutiny; it can take a 'snapshot' of existing outcomes. Applications include the measurement of segregation within cities where, for example, a minority comprising 15 per cent of the total population is not seen as segregated if it comprises 15 per cent of all sub-areas, but is possibly highly segregated if it is present only in some areas, not at all in others. A simple Lorenz curve can be produced by cumulating the percentages of the dominant population type in each city sub-area along one axis of a graph and by cumulating the percentages of the minority along the other. A perfect 45 degree angle is formed if the two groups are equally represented throughout the city and any deviation from this is commonly labelled a 'segregation curve'. It was hoped that such an approach could be applied in this research with the wealthiest and least-wealthy groups being contrasted in their abilities to achieve satisfactory shopping. Whilst a Lorenz approach is certainly more feasible than a Pareto approach certain difficulties can be anticipated. One is that the 'most wealthy' and 'least

15

wealthy' groups are not discrete categories but are arranged along a wealth continuum and no logical sub-divisions come readily to mind. Secondly, and more seriously, the city segregation example outlined above does not measure the differences between the majority and the minority in terms of spatial proximity either to each other, the city centre, or some other spatially-fixed point. This study concerns itself with two firmly fixed spatial points - ASDA, Waterlooville and Havant Hypermarket - and has already established that their respective locations in space are extremely important factors in welfare. Whilst Lorenz approaches may be used to contrast geographically different areas they have no inherent capacity to measure distance as a variable and this may be a fatal weakness. Just as likely to be a limitation on the Lorenz approach is Smith's observation (1977, p.154) that:

"It is assumed that all individuals have
similar preferences."

It became clear that the present study area required somewhat more sophisticated analysis than the crude application of a Pareto or Lorenz approach and indeed the former could be dismissed entirely. Shopping is emerging as a highly complex facet of modern living that can best be addressed at a higher level of resolution than that simply of 'need'. The whole question of location and accessibility has to be handled carefully since the question is not just one of proximity but proximity to what? It has to be established that a nearby retail outlet offers the level of service that individuals demand - or that leaves them not feeling some relative disadvantage. Some observers seem unable to appreciate the concept of relative disadvantage and prefer to believe that the retail market is functioning properly as long as everyone is accessible to some form of shop. It must surely be obvious, however, that for the poorest groups in society it is proximity to stores offering low prices that is important and studies have consistently shown hypermarkets and superstores to offer the lowest prices. Tesco, for example, have a three-tier pricing system and the lowest tier of prices is available only in their superstores. For other groups of people price may be of less significance than convenience, easy parking or quality of goods. In other words there is quite simply no way of expressing the retail demands of diverse groups in terms of the same criteria for all. Satisfaction is a highly individual concept and the approach chosen in this work must be alert to that fact.

Ginsburg (1965, p.73) states:

"There is general agreement that gross inequalities
are unjust, and the right to minimum conditions
of well-being is now widely recognised; but there
is no agreement as to the distribution of
property or the reward of service as above the
minimum."

This is a clear invitation to consider the theories of Simon
(1957) where the concept of 'satisficing' represents a welcome
break from the idea that the same criteria can apply to all
individuals provided the background circumstances are broadly
similar. Applying this to the present study area might permit
one to identify the accessibility of all individuals to all
stores - but require at the same time that an even greater
emphasis be placed on identifying whether or not those stores
are 'satisfactory'.

It may seem that no welfare-based technique is likely to be
adequate for the analysis of the relative disadvantage attendant upon the construction of ASDA Waterlooville and Havant
Hypermarket, but this should not detract from the importance
of a welfare approach. Notions of consumer welfare are an
essential counterbalance to the approach of sales maximisation
whatever the penalties accruing to the marginally, located or
less mobile consumer. All that has been established in effect
is that the shopping opportunities are 'Pareto non-comparable'
(Quirk and Saposnik 1968, p.117); in other words no absolute
standard can be found that will truly apply to all people.
Shopping in its widest sense can only be analysed through
approaches involving concepts of individual behaviour and
preference if all the nuances and shades of opinion are to be
detected. That said, it is still impossible to ignore the
constraint that lack of mobility places on those groups that
are most disadvantaged. The vast majority of individuals in
an area such as south-east Hampshire can experience their
shopping purely in the realms of preference and taste. Others
have to temper this with the constraint that few stores -
possibly only one or two - will be accessible to them. Accessibility as a concept needed to be thoroughly examined and
some assessment made of the ability of individuals to overcome
the frictional effects of distance. For some groups distance
is not a problem but for others it is a major challenge and it
is not difficult to predict which types of people fall into
each category. Harvey (1973, p.82) has stated:

17

"Consider, for example, the ability to think
abstractly about, and to schematise, spatial
relationships - a skill which is closely
correlated with other aspects of intelligence
(Smith, 1964). Such a schematic skill allows
the individual to transcend space and command
it as a resource. Those who lack such a skill
are likely to be trapped by space."

Pahl (1965) has also suggested that the higher-income and
better educated groups tend to make an active use of space,
whereas lower income groups feel trapped by it. The question
is clearly compounded by the issue of the provision of stores
and their specific location, further adding weight to the
significance of this study. On the basis of the observations
made thus far it is clear that the poorer sectors of society
need stores offering low prices to be provided near to them,
yet rarely has this been researched. It also seems inherently
unlikely that such considerations are uppermost in the minds
of retail decision-makers. Before considering the very real
problems associated with the provision of shopping for the
disadvantaged, one further welfare-related approach demanded
consideration. Though the Pareto approach may be dismissed
and the Lorenz approach is severely constrained by the spatial
inputs to the present study, a further general welfare paradigm
may be contemplated. This is the 'social indicator' approach
and it seems likely that it comes as close as any welfare
paradigm to the present requirement to use personal, individual
interpretations as a measure of satisfaction with shopping.
Smith (1979, p.15) has offered a useful summary:

"The subjective approach takes as its implicit point
of departure the proposition that it is how
individuals feel that matters most. Objective
conditions such as housing quality, level of pay,
security on the streets, and services available
affect people's level of life satisfaction or
happiness. Different people, in different
classes and inhabiting different places, can
react differently to the same objective conditions.
This effect is assumed to be measureable, both
with respect to the existing situation and to
the impact of some change that might result
from public policy or private action.

This approach can be viewed as an updated attempt
on the part of social psychologists to solve the
problem of measuring individual 'utility' which
bedevilled welfare economics until theory became so

abstract as not to require any empirical
reference. The subjective approach to social
indicators relies largely on attitudinal survey
instruments, designed to find out how people
view their own life quality and its contributory
'domains', eg. employment, neighbourhood quality
and social services."

Although Smith at no stage mentions shopping, it is clear
that the spirit of the above passage is very close to the
approach required here. If more econometric measures will not
work and, as seems likely, the problems are likely to be idiographic or place-specific, then almost all one is left with
is 'how individuals feel'. Placed more formally, the present
study adopts an approach that is closer to Kirk's (1963)
concept of 'behavioural environment' than his 'objective
environment'. People inhabit their own 'real world' and that
'reality' is what they perceive it to be, their behaviour
following from their conception of reality. Whilst the
majority then operate much as they choose to, some attention
must be paid to those who suffer constraints upon their
actions.

SOURCES OF CONSTRAINT : LOCATION AND ACCESSIBILITY
There are two very good reasons for paying substantial attention to the constrained minority at the expense of the more
liberated majority. One is that an ultimate aim is to produce
policy formulations and this cannot be done if there are as
many potential policies as there are individual demands: some
basic level of provision has to be set. Secondly, such an
approach allows one to at least attempt to draw upon the
existing literature on public service provision, where minimum
standards of provision are a common concern and to focus in on
Hudson's (1980) suggestion that constraints help explain the
gulf between stated preference and observed behaviour.

Because the vital resource of food is not publicly-provided,
this study area has been neglected in comparison with other
fields where public involvement is more direct. One classic
example of the latter, albeit at a more macro-spatial level,
is the study by Townsend and Davidson (1982) on 'Inequalities
in Health' (The Black Report). At a more micro level, Moon
(1982) has studied many aspects of public service provision in
the Borough of Havant - the present study area. Why should
the apparently vital provision of basic foodstuffs be so little
analysed? One reason could be the very low barriers to entry
in the retail trade. Most publicly-provided services tend to
be expensive to organise and supply, or there may be legislation
controlling standards that needs to be centrally administered.

By contrast the retail trade can easily be entered by individuals wishing to provide a service and product standards are readily monitored both at source and by local officials. In short, retail services, despite their essential nature, are felt to be safe in the hands of private entrepreneurs without direct public interference. Also, it is generally evident that in this country at least, the private sector is not ignoring the basic needs of any significant sector of the community. The low barriers to entry mean that it is generally assumed that long before any significant group of people is left totally unserved, a profitable market for a new entrepreneur will appear. It is an interesting observation that Christaller (1933) incorporated a basic welfare concept into his model that no area of his homogeneous plain was to be left unserved.

Merely because no area is left unserved, does not imply that all areas are equally well served, and rural areas are a case in point (Moseley, 1979). Much recent work has demonstrated that new markets are appearing in the suburbs to which entrepreneurs are presently being drawn. There are two major fields of relevant research here; one is the identification of the consumer groups that are likely to be disadvantaged by such a trend. Another concerns the proper means of the expression of that disadvantage. Since neither has been adequately discussed with reference to store types in the past, the present thesis seeks to remedy this. Background material on the dimensions of the welfare issue will first be outlined and then the various sub-groups most involved will be analysed.

GENERAL WELFARE ISSUES
What is immediately apparent from the literature is that disparities in the ability to acquire basic needs are all too evident in modern British society. Field (1979) has suggested that, in 1976, the top five per cent of British society held 62 per cent of the total wealth. Definitions of poverty have fluctuated through time, but at present many millions of British residents are subjected to the 'poverty trap'. There are obvious implications of this for the provision and purchase of essentials such as food. It cannot generally be suggested that the poorer British consumer faces all of the problems outlined in the American context by Caplowitz (1967). The extension of credit for food purchasing, and the attendant higher costs, is not a prevalent practice in Britain. It is evident, however, that some of the poorer sectors of society are forced to use nearby, and often more expensive shops. The two key consequences of this appear to be those of inferior quality goods and the unavailability of bulk purchasing opportunities. Note, too, that bulk purchases need a larger financial outlay which the poorer consumer may not be able to meet.

20

Food shopping dominates the expenditure patterns of the poor. This is confirmed by Central Statistical Office figures which indicate that in 1982 the greatest single share of all consumers' expenditure was taken by food at 16.9 percent and the figure is far higher for the poorer groups. The essential geographical input here is that if the poor are at a minimal distance from their ideal shopping then the spatial disadvantage is minimised.

By extension, Hillman (1973) drew upon research into car ownership patterns to present a wide-ranging case against hypermarkets. Indeed, this study in part constitutes an empirical test of the work of Hillman since he claims that whilst some sectors of the community will doubtless benefit from these large new stores, others may find that the new competition has forced their local shops out of business, leaving them with longer journeys. Hillman's arguments were apparently rebutted by Kirby (1975) on the evidence of experience in the United States but though local shopping may not actually be lost, it has already been seen that the advantages of shopping in large new stores are still not available to the less mobile. Thus, whilst they may not lose their local shopping, neither do they gain, and so they suffer relative disadvantage. Furthermore, it is the view of Hillman that shopping is commonly undertaken in association "with other trips, such as ..... going to the library ..... and so on" (1973, p.91). If this can be proven to be the case, then hypermarket shopping, in locations which are far distant from other services, carries inherent disadvantages. Hillman's comment further invites inspection of the social function of shopping and it is a major aim of the present study to outline the extent to which food shopping may be undertaken along with other shopping. With specific regard to shopping and income Guy (1983, p.1) states:

"Household income is clearly an important influence
on food shopping - directly through its relationship with expenditure, and indirectly - through its
influence on car ownership, freezer ownership etc."

What emerged from Guy's study of Cardiff in 1982 was that expenditure relates to family size and income levels. His results showed that it was the highest income groups that used superstores the most. An inverse relationship was identifiable for the smaller, more numerous, more accessible superettes, where 48.9 per cent of those with an income under £3,000 used such stores. Guy himself (1983, p.3) commented:

"These figures... are affected by the accessibility
of these store types."

This is precisely the point that the present study set out to
investigate and, though tangential to Guy's interests, a key
premise of this study is that sections of the community who
most need large stores are least likely to gain advantage from
them if they are placed in inaccessible locations. Already
there is evidence to show that social class measures, often as
income surrogates, are important in retail studies. Potter
(1976, p.491-2) notes:

"Variations in the number of centres in the
information field, the mean distance of such
centres from the consumer and the angular
extent of the field within the town were all
shown to be closely related to social class
variability amongst consumers."

In aggregate, existing research has pointed in three direc-
tions: to the effects of accessibility *per se*; to the effects
of income differences and to the possible effects of new stores
on small shops. Accessibility is a key topic to be taken
further and it will certainly be necessary to discover which
groups in the study area are most likely to suffer disadvantage.
The only key thrust of research that is not seen as crucial is
the role of the small shop: firstly, because the effects of
competition on other traders are not a central concern and
secondly, because polarisation theory (Kirby, 1976) suggests
that small shops may thrive on the top-up trade from hypermarkets. What should be noted is that the superstore and the
hypermarket have tended, as in the case of the Tesco operation,
to lead to a reduction in the numbers of supermarkets. Supermarkets may not be as price-competitive as superstores but
they have for many years provided low-income families with a
nearby shopping opportunity that offers prices lower than the
corner shop and which stocks a fairly wide range of goods.
Quite simply, both the superstore and the hypermarket threaten
the type of store upon which the most constrained households
have come to rely. This is yet another reason why they should
be located where such households can reach them.

ACCESSIBILITY
It was important to consider existing evidence of poor retail
provision or of factors that might give rise to differential
abilities to reach local shopping opportunities. Many of
the studies so far considered made much of the issue of simple
accessibility, the ability to overcome the frictional effects
of distance. Initially one could consider some of the general

dimensions of the accessibility problem. As Coates, Johnston and Knox (1977, p.181) state:

"Distance is a barrier; it takes time and money to cross it, so that it inhibits the flow of information, especially that which involves personal experience rather than propagation through the telecommunications of mass media. Because of this barrier, people living in different places have different levels of accessibility to jobs, to housing opportunities, to shops, police stations, hospitals, reference groups, and so on. Some of these variations in accessibility produce spatial variations in monetary values, in the price which labour can command, and which is asked for housing and various consumer goods. They can also produce variations in what we call real income, the sum of the various components which comprise a level of living. Residents of certain places must pay extra costs to attend certain facilities, because of the travel involved; if the distances are too great, they may have to go without altogether."

In one of the more significant works on transport and accessibility, Hillman *et al* (1976) focused on household car ownership. They noted that many adults cannot drive, though they may well live in car-owning households. They showed that in their five study areas, licence owning ranged from 48 per cent upwards among men in contrast to 38 per cent downwards among women.

Hillman *et al* illustrated the problem of low levels of driving licence-holding and suggest that car-based shopping is open to fewer people than might at first appear to be the case. In the context of this thesis, particular note was made of Hillman's evidence that many women in suburban locations had neither a car nor a driving licence.

When the purpose of the journey was taken into account it became apparent that shopping is "principally done on foot" (Hillman *et al* (1976 p.7) though what this does not reveal is the extent to which the volume of shopping is done on foot or by other means. The short distance, frequent 'topping up' visit on foot may be a direct consequence of the monthly trip to a hypermarket by car, but the latter may account for fifty times more expenditure or volume of goods purchased. It was not feasible to undertake such a major survey in this study as

23

that required to catalogue every shopping purchase for large groups of people. Guy *et al* (1983) have produced such a study for the Cardiff area, however, and some reference has already been made to this study.

Several researchers have shown that car availability and licence holding are interrelated with other wider factors. Even variability in housing type (Nader, 1969) may be a sufficient catch-all to identify groups whose overall social and economic characteristics vary greatly. Potter (1980) has shown the close relationship between, for example, social class and car availability for shopping. Additionally, the particular problems of the elderly have been emphasised by the work of Moseley (1979). For example, whilst noting that 85 per cent of British people over retirement age have a bus concession this does not imply that bus transport is straightforward. Moseley notes (1979 pp.6-47):

"Even if a bus service runs quite near an elderly person's home, this does not mean that all is well. A five minute walk can be exhausting and elderly people have even greater difficulty returning from the bus stop after a tiring journey and with heavy shopping bags."

Moseley saw problems cumulating for the elderly as 'multiple mobility deprivation' and problems of this sort should not be overlooked even in a suburban context. Probably the most useful concepts lie in the overall field of "time geography" (Moseley 1979 pp.66-69), where access itself is measured and space is viewed as a constraint. One has to concede that even transport on foot over short distances can pose problems, and evidence exists on such problems for young women with children (as provided by Hillman 1976 p.52). It is clear that this group shares with the elderly some real mobility problems, as Table 2.1 fully demonstrates.

What is equally evident is that bus transport, too, may pose great problems for this sector of the community and a disaggregation of mobility of data by social group has been given by Mitchell and Town (1977). The modal split for their shopping groups showed that 'D' social group shoppers were nearly three times less likely to shop by car than were 'A' social group shoppers. Their use of two contrasted classes in the Social Class spectrum (A and D) illustrated very well the contrasts that emerge when such data are disaggregated.

Table 2.1
Transport problems for women with children

Group characteristics

	Women travelling with children when youngest child is:			Women travelling alone	
	under three	three to four	five and over		
proportion of group with transport problems	% 42	% 36	% 27	% 29	percentage
	118	78	161	357	totals
Of those with problems, the problem is due to:	%	%	%		
traffic/crossing roads	38	53	39		
narrow pavement	32	14	21		
uneven pavement	21	9	15		
hills/ramps	14	7	14		
no pavement	12	26	16		
mud/grass pavement	8	12	8		
kerbs/steps	8	2	2		
places too far away	6	5	7		
other	17	14	19		
total with problems	77	43	103		

Source: Hillman (1976)

Pickup (1981) has presented a series of useful tables outlining the relationship between shopping and household mobility. For example, they show data based on results from the National Travel Survey, with licence-holding disaggregated by age group. It is clear that licence-holding among women is increasing and that among younger age groups the gap between men and women is closing.

Other evidence reveals the expected relationship between licence holding and the number of cars in the household. There is clear evidence that areas of two car ownership are likely to be source regions for women well able to make use of car-based shopping facilities. Further cross-tabulation revealed that 90 percent of householders in the 30-39 age group and in two car households themselves held full driving licences. By contrast, only 27 percent of housewives who were aged 50-59 and who lived in one car households also held a full driving licence. The importance of late-night shopping was also emphasised since one can reasonably assume that shopping journeys are postponed until the household car is available. Pickup suggested that longer journeys were also postponed and noted that womens' journeys as a car passenger doubled after 5.00 pm. For working women, Daws and Bruce (1971), too, found a rise in later shopping trips.

It should not be forgotten that the family car need not always be used by the family wage-earner as the means of journey to work, since the housewife/shopper may be left with the car to use for shopping purposes. A local parallel to this is found in the Gosport area where there is a very low incidence of two car households. There is a high proportion of naval personnel and the housewife may have exclusive use of the family car for extended periods while the husband is away at sea. Bruce and Delworth (1976) produced data indicating the extent to which housewives may have access to a car, as driver or passenger, by different times of day and day of the week. Note that the practice of offering lifts may bring car-based shopping within the purview of non-car households. Bruce and Delworth also emphasise the dominance (in terms of frequency) of the short walk to the local shop and National Travel Survey data similarly reveal half of all shopping stages to be less than 1.6 kms and, of those, 95 percent are undertaken on foot. This should not be taken to mean that ideal shopping facilities are so readily accessible. For example, Guy's study of Reading (1976) found that 90 percent of households in his survey area had access to all basic foodstores within walking distance of home. When supermarkets - which have been identified as important to low-income groups - are the focus of interest, however, Bowlby (1979) found only 21 percent of housewives in Oxford so served. What does become apparent from all these studies is that with the availability of a car, the number of shopping trips decreases. This implies a greater volume of purchases per trip, confirming the use of the car as a mobile shopping basket.

A problem with mobility data is that they are often presented at too general a scale. Hallsworth (1985c) has shown that though the national pattern of car ownership shows generally higher levels in the south, marked variations occur when data are spatially disaggregated. Thus whilst Hampshire as a whole records car ownership figures well above the national average, six inner city enumeration districts in Portsmouth were shown by the 1981 Census of Population to have over 80 percent of households without a car.

SHOPPING AND GENDER

Bowlby (1981) has suggested that despite claims that the retail system offers opportunity for more efficient shopping, the amount of time spent on shopping has not radically decreased. It is suggested that shopping, and hence providing for the family, has in fact become reinforced as a 'housewifely duty' and is a suitable and justifiable way to spend time. Even employed women seem to share this pressure though they may have less time to devote to shopping. This leads back to the concept of shopping as a 'social activity' and the actions a housewife has to take to be, or be seen to be, the 'caring provider'. Bruce and Delworth (1976, p.33) found that the preferred type of centre for food shopping had more than one supermarket. This raises the possibility of price-comparison or 'shopping around' as a significant part of the shopping process. Furthermore, as 50 percent of women are in paid employment, Bowlby suggests that shopping opportunities close to the workplace might be an asset.

Clearly, the gender aspect brings one back to social or non-economic aspects and note may be made of the work of Hoggart (1978) who, in a small sample of North Yorkshire households, analysed a five-fold split of consumer types. Broadly based on the work of Stone (1954), Hoggart's classification was of Apathetic, Constrained, Contented, Economic and Personalising consumers. Hoggart uses the evidence of Rich and Jain (1968) and Aburn (1973) to cast doubt on the effectiveness of socio-economic variables alone in determining shopping behaviour. Hoggart notes that shopping not involving travel, ie. having goods delivered, may be a possible strategem for some. He notes (1978, p.421), "As might be expected, constrained consumers undertook significantly fewer shopping trips over the study month than any other consumer type." With direct

27

reference to consumer income differences one may note the work of Davies (1968) who studied two small areas in Leeds where, he believed, income factors might be isolated from all others. One area was a local authority 'council' estate, the other a peripheral private housing area, each with its own shopping complex. Davies' prime aim was to study the interrelationship between the local area and the type and functional diversity of the shops within its area. He concluded that the higher income area was more functionally specialised compared with the more broadly based spectrum of goods and services offered by shops in the low income area. In the same study region, Davies (1969) went on to analyse consumer shopping behaviour and found that the high income area generated a greater demand for services and what might be termed luxury goods in general, in line with what might be expected. More importantly, he found (1969, p.117) that "81 percent of shoppers in Middleton (the low income area) frequent stores in the area for groceries as against 57 percent in Street Lane".

There is evidence, then, of the operation of constraints and Davies confirmed that the lower income residents are more likely to use "chain stores and general stores". His overall conclusion was that "The higher income levels of shoppers in Street Lane allow for much greater freedom of mobility" stating that this has "significant ramifications for store location planning" (1969 p.117).

In a similar vein to Bowlby, Tivers (1977) identified the gender role constraint as a major influence on the spatial activity patterns of women. Their likely activities were constrained by the roles they were expected to play and it is obvious that shopping is one of these roles (see Tivers 1977, p.23). Having already seen that women have less access to cars and to licences we can conclude that they are doubly constrained as the role of shopping is delegated in many cases to those whose ability to overcome the friction of distance is least. What cannot now be ignored is the attitudes that women, and particularly housewives, have towards shopping. They would seem to be emerging as a key group, for as Town (1980, p.10) notes:

"Shopping is an activity in which almost all
the population is involved at least once a
week. The highest journey rate is that of
housewives who, in 1975/6 made 77 percent
more journeys for this purpose than the
population as a whole."

Disaggregation of accessibility-related factors is again important and, finally, Bruce has attempted to provide a general
framework for non-economic approaches to shopping, stating:

"The subject of human factors in shopping
provision can be put roughly under three
general headings termed here as cultural,
individual and perceptual" (1974, p.280).

To Bruce, cultural factors would subsume both 'housewifely'
roles and the use of shopping as social interaction. The
individual factors would deal with preferences at the level of
the individual; for example, for 'shopping around' or for
one-stop-shopping. The perceptual concentrates on issues,
for example, of store image and all these factors are to be
taken into account, building on the work of Bruce (1974) and
Bowlby (1979).

MANAGERIALISM
The link between welfare criteria and the possible agents of
welfare-related change is extremely strong and attention must
now be paid to the question of how best to conceptualise the
role of those agents. They may be key figures in retailing
but the prime agents must be the planners since they will be
expected to administer any statements on retail policy.
Smith (1977, p.159) has observed:

"As who gets what, where, becomes increasingly a
matter of deliberate public choice in many
countries, it is important that the planning
process is explicitly recognised as a means of
redressing existing inequalities in the spatial
distribution of human life chances."

Numerous other authors have discussed the role of planners
and Harvey has suggested that the very act of prediction - or
planning in its broadest sense - is bound to influence eventual
outcomes. He sees (1973, p.51) that planners are "inextricably
bound up with the social processes generating change" claiming
that published plans are certain to influence the course of
events and may even be self-fulfilling. An example of this
type of situation exists in the study area where a shortage of
land for purpose-built factories is experienced. Yet the
reality is that there is no shortage of land that has been
zoned for industry by planners and the shortage occurs because
once industrial areas were announced they were purchased specu-
latively as developments for factory rental. Property for
rental is preferred by institutions but entrepreneurs prefer to
buy. Had planners not declared certain areas to be industrial

zones but instead released land as demand grew, then the present problem would not exist. It follows that planners can exert influence almost as a by-product of general planning statments and that policies directed to a particular topic - such as retailing - can be expected to be very influential. Hall (1974, p.272) believes the planner to be "in a state of continuous interaction with the system he is planning, a system that changes partly, but not entirely, due to processes beyond his mechanisms of control". Most of the pressures for retail change have been outlined in chapter two and matters of planning control require equal attention.

It is useful at this point to note that land-use planning in Britain is generally regarded as having a more powerful influence than in, for example, the United States, though its influence is less marked than in some European countries. Many people firmly believe that planners exert real influence on retail outcomes, and NEDO (1971, p.5) stated, "Rightly or wrongly, the impression is widely held that central government and local planning authorities hold an adverse attitude to (hypermarkets)". If planners genuinely do have a 'corporate ethic' that causes them to tend to shun certain sorts of retail forms then this will certainly emerge as ASDA Waterlooville and Havant Hypermarket are discussed in turn. The priority was to discover if there is a way of conceptualising the role of planners as a group and attention is now paid to the work of Raymond Pahl.

Pahl and managerialism
Pahl (1975, pp.249-250) has demonstrated the role of individuals whom he describes as 'managers of the urban system' with empirical evidence drawn from Eastern Europe, where resources are far more likely to be 'allocated' rather than 'competed for' under conditions of free market choice. Pahl demonstrated parallel situations where, in western societies, individual choice was similarly circumscribed and it was again more appropriate to think in terms of 'allocation' of resources. His starting point was the provision of scarce urban resources where problems of accessibility ensued - in line with the subject of this thesis. Pahl also identified constraints on access that are social, not spatial, and reflect "the distribution of power in society" (Pahl 1975, p.201). Pahl's formulations have a clear geographical input since he writes of resources located in space and of the constraints (spatial or social) on access to them. For present purposes it is intuitively attractive to see planners, and possibly other powerful figures, as managers of the urban system and to cast their roles accordingly. It should be noted that Pahl's work is not without its critics and Pahl himself (1970, p.282) refuses to make dogmatic statements about the precise role of managers:

30

"There is considerable difficulty in determining
whether, in specific instances, a policy is
progressive or regressive in its effects.... it
cannot be easily determined whether the 'managers
of the urban system' are the agents of the national
or local political system, advocates of the poor
in their locality, or operators of some abstract
professional principles, the distributional effects
of which are not known in detail, if at all."

So, whilst the theories clearly have relevance, there is some
fluidity in interpretation and much of this relates to the
changing role of the urban manager at various levels of the
bureaucratic hierarchy. The true power wielded by a Whitehall
senior civil servant and a local junior planner will surely be
different. Indeed, Pahl went on to outline four possible conceptualisations of managerialism, each dependent upon one's
over-arching view of control in society. He has conceded that
managerialism might be seen as a tool for attacking the middle
levels of bureaucracy rather than for tackling issues related
to society at large.

It is clear that central to the whole managerialist issue is
the extent to which the urban manager or gatekeeper enjoys
autonomy. In certain circumstances, most classically in the
bureaucracy surrounding the allocation of local authority
housing, the managerialist propositions might seem to hold up
well. In such a case the gatekeeper has effective control of
the resource that is to be allocated, since it is locally
provided. In the case of retailing, however, the resources -
being large new retail outlets - are not provided by the
planners themselves as 'gatekeepers'. Furthermore, the gatekeepers have little power even to encourage the initiation
of such facilities. Under the present planning system, the
Planning or Development Control Officer cannot instruct or
direct a retail chain to provide a specific level of services
in a specific location. Indeed, planning is characterised as
'negative' or 'planning by response' to outside initiatives.
This managerialist stance is thus well removed from that prevailing in the housing office, primarily because the resource
to be allocated is externally provided. Nevertheless, planners
remain the key regulatory figures and the final chapter accordingly addresses policy implications.

The work of a number of researchers helped to clarify these
issues and many of the possible managerialist approaches were
examined by Moon (1982). He sought to examine bureaucratic
influence in Havant borough as a core hypothesis, with auxiliary
hypotheses of electoral and structural effects. In the case

31

of Moon's work, however, the emphasis was firmly placed at
local level, whereas in the present study the key influences
may be at a higher level. At the local level, Moon (1982,
p.237) was able to state "primacy of the bureaucracy.... was
vindicated". It is vital to note that Moon found Development
Control, the area relevant to this study, was more influenced
by structuralist forces. It will clearly be necessary to
examine planning-based influences on the present study area
at all levels. As a guideline Guy (1980) suggested that
councillors generally adopt attitudes similar to those of
planners and that these attitudes emerge as policy guidelines.

Pahl's work reformulated
Norman (1975) notes that Pahl reformulated his own work such
that the term "manager" applied only to officials of local
government and goes on to discuss recent examples of managerialist approaches. He notes (1975, p.14):

> "Pahl allows that the managers play a crucial
> mediating role between the state and private
> sector and between external state authority and
> the local population and goes on ... "Clearly
> then we are looking for the boundaries of a group
> of occupations which are not occupations of the
> capitalist economic system itself ... we are
> looking for occupations which play a mediating
> role ... the broad range of agencies of the
> 'welfare state' in the British situation are the
> obvious first candidates as 'managers'". But taken
> literally this leads to some surprising bedfellows.
> Housing manager and planners will be top of
> everybody's list."

Norman clearly feels that both private and public occupations
may fulfill the mediating role. What is notable here is that
the present objects of interest, the planners, are seen as
falling into the mediating function and thus are a suitable
case for a managerialist analysis. What may be left open as
an issue is the question, as posed by Pahl (1975, p.87), "who
manages the managers?" In some ways this comment can be seen
as predicting the inevitable debate between proponents of the
managerialist viewpoint and those, notably basing their work
on the theories of Castells, whose analyses are more radical.

Fortunately, Leonard (1982) has turned attention to the relationship between managerialist theory and Marxist political
economy interpretations of society. He specifically addresses
the claims of the latter that the former lacks universality.
Leonard attempts to show how managerialism can have wider
applicability and concludes (1982, p.202):

32

"Pahl's Weberian analysis has, as has been shown, drawn upon corporatism to extend its value to macro-economic situations, whilst Marxism responds by seeing no reason to assume that the hegemony of private capital has been undermined."

Leonard concedes that local managerial autonomy can be doubly constrained since real managerial power may rest at a higher bureaucratic level while the local planner is also restricted in his actions by politically-elected committee members. This may result possibly in such powerlessness among certain managers that the system can only be viewed, as it were, at a higher level of resolution such as proposed by the structuralists. This proposition has been discussed, notably by Williams (1978), Leonard (1979) and Pahl (1979), and again one has to decide if managerialism is a worthwhile paradigm. To turn the argument around, Johnston (1980), in criticism of structuralists, argues firmly that their chosen scale of resolution is so 'macro' as to preclude any geographically-based analyses. Johnston's call (1980, p.411) is for, "positivist/behavioural approaches within modern geography" and this is a viewpoint adopted within this study. Structuralists have little time for empirical, geographically-based approaches yet it will be demonstrated that real inequalities can be found within the urban system that could be within the power of local 'managers' to redress, irrespective of the wider forces at work in society. Kirby (1981) has also called for geographers to study 'place poverty' - those deprived 'in situ' and, furthermore, has also sought to show that the gap between the structuralists and those who wish to undertake spatially-based micro-level analyses is not as great at it might seem. Though earlier writings of Castells appeared to downplay a spatial emphasis, Kirby (1981, p.180) finds encouragement in this passage:

"... it seems that the traditional inequality in terms of incomes, which is inherent in capitalism, is expressed in new social cleavages related to the accessibility and use of certain collective services, from housing conditions to working hours, passing through the type and level of health, educational and cultural facilities... there is a new source of inequality inherent in the very use of these collective goods which have become a fundamental part of the daily consumption pattern." (Castells, 1978, pp.15-16).

This seems to take us back to an interest in accessibility, a truly central factor here, and it also takes us forward into the structuralist emphasis on collective consumption. An interest that, as Saunders (1983) notes, is far from resolved in the structuralist debate. Harvey (1981, p.96) has referred to "the built environment for consumption" whilst Saunders himself points out the contrast between Lojkine's 1976 view that: "The mode of consumption is collective and is thus by its nature opposed to individual private appropriation. Parks or lessons cannot be consumed individually - at least, not in their current increasingly socialized form", and that of Castells which defines collective consumption in terms of the nature of the provision of facilities.

The contrast between provision and use suggests the need for empirical work in this field by the structuralists themselves. Certainly Harris (1983) has no difficulty in defending a spatial approach and Castells himself (1983, p.3) has since stated:

"Years ago I criticized such a concept and
showed that spatial forms do not determine
social relationships (Castells 1972); rather
they intervene in a complex network of variables,
which are fundamentally dominated by relations
of production, gender, and power (Castells 1983).
Yet from the critique of the 'spatialist theory'
of social crises, it does not follow that space
is unimportant and that the spatial dimension of
the crisis should be ignored. Indeed, quite the
contrary holds: societies exist only in time and
space."

Whilst being mindful of the critiques by Eyles and Lee (1982) and Silk (1982), it is the approach postulated by Johnston that will be adhered to in this study. Cullen (1980) gives concrete evidence that a worthwhile managerialist analysis of planners can be made. Cullen accepts Pahl's proposition that it is the results of managerialism that should concern us but rejects what he sees as Pahl's retreat from his own theories when apparently losing interest in middle-ranking planners. Cullen states (1980, p.268):

"Whether the motivation for channelling urban
resources in a certain way stems more from
national government or the intermediate middle
men, if the aims and values of both are synony-
mous, then the results remain the same."

Cullen goes on to suggest that when treated as a group, planners see national government at the top of the power hierarchy as regards allocation and distribution of resources. This can only have increased with the highly-centralist policies of the present Thatcher government. However, Cullen claims (1980, p.280):

"In the final encounter between ideas and their
practical implementation, planners are those
who control development at grass roots level,
dictate the realities of day-to-day construction
and destruction, and who prepare and implement
far-reaching developments which effect the
destiny of whole areas."

In the context of this study the 'far reaching developments' can be taken as structure plan policies for retailing.

Cullen found evidence of the pre-eminence of managerialism and a final reference to the work of Cullen serves to emphasise the importance of this in the present study. He asked planners to rank 'quality of life' priorities for two class-stereotypes. Though the ranking of a golf course varied considerably depending upon the stereotype, the provision of a supermarket was ordered as first priority for 'working class' and priority two – second only to 'Parks and Green space' – for 'middle class' groups. Yet again, the importance of retailing is emphasised but gives rise to two further questions. How does one reconcile the fact that the retail planner cannot control the new inputs to the system? What evidence exists of planner/retailer interaction? The solution to the first question lies, in this work, with a brief consideration of the motives of the retailers as well as consideration of the planners as urban managers. What is exceedingly useful is that during the period of development of ASDA, Waterlooville and Havant Hypermarket the retailers themselves began to seek a dialogue with planners and also to widely publicise their trading philosophies. As a result, clear insights were gained into the trading philosophies of some retailers since Tesco, for example, began to publish their policy statements. It is to these revelations on trading philosophy that attention now turns and the case study of Asda is taken since this company owns one of the stores under consideration and has also been very active in promoting its trading philosophy.

THE RETAILERS (THE EXAMPLE OF ASDA)
It is especially useful to look closely at the types of official statement that the ASDA group was making about itself in the 1970s. Ridgway (1976, pp.24-35) stated, for example,

35

"during recent years my company has worked closely with many
authorities in connection with District Centres.... I am glad
to say that all of them to date have been singularly successful."
This is a statement of trader cooperation, rather than confron-
tation, with planners and Ridgway in the same paper states his
company's apparent concern for the "underprivileged" noting
that free bus services and extra facilities for the elderly
and disabled are a feature of their stores. When Ridgway
retired as Development Director of ASDA his successor, D.
Gransby, took on the role of explaining the ASDA philosophy on
trading, for example, (1984, p.47):

"There are few Local Authorities around today
with a blanket 'no-superstores' policy.
Adopting such a line in an area where the need
for a superstore can be demonstrated allows a
superstore operator to win a site on appeal.
In this way the Council gets the unwanted gift
of a superstore on possibly not the best site
as far as it is concerned. This is not the way
to plan. A more professional and objective
approach, in my view, is for a Local Authority
to examine its area to determine need - perhaps
in consultation with superstore operators and if
one or more superstores need to be accommodated,
to decide where in a town the community would
most benefit from a superstore and how it can
help to achieve other objectives within a Local
Plan. The merits of each superstore proposal
would be assessed using standard planning criteria
and judged accordingly. These criteria, however,
must include commercial parameters, ie. the
operational and locational need of the superstore
operator must be recognised."

It is clear from Gransby's ensuing comments that a process of
co-operative interchange of ideas between planner and developer
reduces uncertainty as to outcomes and assists the entrepreneur
in making investment judgements. Those very judgements also
cast the entrepreneur in the managerialist mould. Finney
(1976) offers evidence of the planner's viewpoint on such
cooperation and quotes the situation whereby his planning
authority could perceive the need for new retail facilities in
a district centre context (Holt Park Village, Leeds) and was
sufficiently flexible to allow a superstore of viable size to
fill the role. This is a type of case study that will need to
be examined later and the planning viewpoint in this case was
to show (Finney 1976, p.49):

36

> "that it is not impossible to provide a type of
> shopping development which major retailers wish
> to pursue and indeed which many members of the
> community wish to use, together with social
> facilities, schools, libraries, health centres
> and so on."

This again seems to emphasise Hillman's point that shopping for goods and services may go hand in hand with the use of other facilities. Also it emphasises the validity of examining shopping as a topic in the same general context of essential provision that society accords to publicly-provided goods and services. The value of Finney's work lies in its consideration of the precise suitability of individual sites for superstore purposes. Finney (1976, p.49) states:

> "I think that it will be possible in many cases
> to find sites which do overcome (these)
> difficulties and will enable the concept of a
> lively retailing/social centre to continue."

In a later article, Ridgway (1981a) states:

> "The enormous popularity with the shopping
> public of these earliest (ASDA) stores led
> planners and Chambers of Trade to believe that
> they would ruin existing town centre shopping
> developments. This antipathy to such new
> shopping developments as exemplified by
> superstores was at its height during the early
> seventies when superstore retailers such as
> ourselves had to seek locations more acceptable
> to the planning authorities...
>
> .... it soon became clear ... that other
> opportunities must be available ... where the
> dynamism of superstore development funded by
> private capital could transform areas both
> economically and socially."

Ridgway goes on to give many examples of superstore developments by ASDA and articles by Ridgway are doubly useful as they give insight into company policy and also show that some retailers at least believe that planners wield a significant amount of power.

It is therefore abundantly evident that if both planner and retailer perform managerialist roles then the interface between them must be explored and the present study area is ideal for

37

this purpose. Although there is now evidence that retail organisations see planners as key elements in the development process, one is still left with the evidence that there are higher ie. governmental, influences if not higher co-ordinated policies. Analysis would certainly be simpler if government policy were more explicitly stated and Davies (1984), Dawson (1980), Mills (1974) and Jones (1979) have noted the lack of a comprehensive retail policy, and the problems that ensue. In the final section of this chapter an attempt is made to briefly assess the framework within which planners work.

THE PLANNING ETHOS
This work is not a study of the spirit and purpose of planning - a topic well covered in numerous publications including Cullingworth (1972) and Hall (1974). Accordingly, only a brief introduction is offered which is intended to show whether or not the earlier comments - attributing to planners a negative attitude towards out-of-town stores - are consistent with an expected viewpoint based on consensus analysis of planning in general in the post-war period. Scrutiny of any of the standard planning texts confirms that indeed this is the case. Hall *et al* (1973) have stated that crucial themes of the 1947 Town and Country Planning Act were urban containment, protection of the countryside and creation of balanced communities. A presumption against decentralised retailing would be entirely consistent with the first two of those aims and also very probably the third. It can be claimed that the 1947 Act was in part a reaction against the suburban sprawl of the 1930s and partly a reaction against urban blight of the nineteenth century. Hall (1974, pp.100-124) discusses the creation of the post-war 'Planning Machine' and his verdict (1974, pp.122-124) emphasises the negative aspects of planning - the aspects of control.

In seeking a direct link to retail aspects of planning, some mention must be made of the concept of hierarchy - drawn from Central Place Theory. It is perhaps inevitable that the orderliness of hierarchical systems should be attractive to planners, especially since many are trained geographers. There is a logical framework for planning decisions, based on trade area data, that helps to underpin planning policies. Hypermarkets do not fit easily within such a schema, and Davies and Sparks (1981) have debated whether or not they should be seen as an entirely new level of provision. What is of significance here is that the hierarchy is accepted and acted upon by planners, rather than the advisability of such a view. Certainly Schiller (1979, p.10) takes issue with planners over their acceptance of the concept:

"... most planners have been taught Central Place Theory at college and consider it a valuable organisational framework for the control of shopping facilities. The freestanding, non-central superstore does not fit into the hierarchy at all ... a whole series of new County Structure Plans have been published. In the majority of these it is stated as a goal in itself that the existing hierarchy should be reinforced."

Schiller recognises the trend to accommodate superstores in District Centres but states (1979, p.11):

"They are considered unsatisfactory by retailer, planner and shopper alike."

This is not a view accepted in this study, which aims to shed light on Schiller's proposition.

It is clear that their relationship to theories of hierarchy is regarded by Schiller as just about the only virtue of District Centres. If this is so then Central Place Theory carries with it a powerful, if indirect, legacy. From Schiller's viewpoint new District Centres based on superstores are simply a mechanism for making superstore development acceptable and it is clear that the efficacy of adding superstores to District Centres is a prime concern for retail planning.

CONCLUSION
This chapter has ranged widely over such topics as driving licence holding and 'social' aspects of shopping in order to demonstrate the diverse inputs to the concept of 'relative disadvantage' in a retail context. Ultimately, a 'subjective social indicators' approach has come to be seen as the most fruitful avenue for a welfare analysis of food shopping. Further consideration having been given to the over-arching concept of 'control', a managerialist perspective has emerged as most promising and the implication of this will be explored later. The welfare themes will be brought out in Chapters 4, 5 and 6 as evidence accumulates on the key dimensions of 'disadvantage'. As yet, no practical techniques for investigating these varied themes have been brought forward and so these are explored in the following chapter.

3 Research techniques for a welfare geography of retailing

INTRODUCTION

It is now essential to examine previous geographical approaches to the problems of retailing in order to decide upon precise techniques for tackling the welfare issues raised in this study. Geographers have broadly worked within three areas of study when analysing retail-related topics. These areas are Central Place Theory, behavioural approaches, and log-linear modelling; though the three cannot be seen as mutually exclusive. The preceding chapter, on welfare in general, has shown that the behavioural approach seems likely to be the most fruitful given the peculiar problems of the topic under consideration. Central Place Theory shares with the structuralist paradigm the handicap of being cast at a somewhat too 'macro' level of resolution. This study does not concern itself primarily with aspects of the size and placing of urban centres but with the behaviour patterns of individual consumers. The log-linear modelling approach is tangential in that, whilst it has been applied to large foodstores, few attempts have been made to incorporate behavioural aspects though these are being worked upon, as by Cadwallader (1981). Instead, it is upon the substantial body of existing literature on behavioural aspects of retail geography that attention may most usefully be focussed.

BEHAVIOURAL ANALYSES

Shepherd and Thomas (1980) have presented a useful resume of
the types of issues they feel geographers could be tackling
within a general 'behavioural' approach: one of these is a
consideration of 'the spatially disadvantaged consumer', another
is 'examination of the social meanings attached to shopping'.
Both place the present study firmly in the arena of behavioural
approaches as they define it. It is evident that many key
behavioural aspects of shopping are best uncovered by comprehensive analysis of shopper behaviour and the 1982 Cardiff
consumer study undertaken by Wrigley and Guy is especially to
be welcomed. The implication for this work is that as comprehensive an analysis as possible must be made of the shopping
habits of residents of Havant Borough. Once it is accepted
that shoppers do not frequent the shopping opportunity that
is physically nearest to them - and this has been demonstrated
by many studies including Clark and Rushton (1970) and Fingleton
(1975) - then aspects of preference clearly come into play as
Ambrose (1967, p.331) suggests:

"In addition, there may be some unconscious
element of rationalisation involved in the
case of such personal services as hairdressing.
The declared nearest outlet may perhaps be
further away than a hairdressing service which
the respondent has instinctively dismissed as
quite unsuitable."

Warnes and Daniels (1978) have further refined the concept of
nearness as involving that centre with the desired type,
quality and combination of goods and services. This calls for
techniques that are capable of measuring subtleties of individual choice and preference. Potter (1979a, 1982) combines the
key aspects of information and behaviour in an integrated
model. He notes (1982,p.145);

"A given consumer will be aware of a finite
number of retail locations. This set of
centres comprises the information field
of the consumer. Amongst this range of
opportunities, a certain number of centres
will be visited in order to do shopping."

Potter presents a comprehensive analysis of consumer usage and
information fields. Of interest for present purposes is his
analysis of various sub-groups, where it emerges that socio-
economic groups vary in the size and complexity of their information fields. (Potter 1982, p.151).

An important early example of attempts by students of the retail scene to apply techniques of cognitive evaluation was the study by Downs (1970) of the city centre of Bristol. In fact the choice of the study area is revealing, for his initial intention was to study three local shopping centres. This had to be abandoned since it was not possible to obtain a collective image of the three centres among all the respondents. That is, they tended to use only specific parts of the shopping centres and failed to recognise the totality of the centres as perceived by Downs himself. Downs finally analysed the Broadmead shopping centre on which a consensus of "imageability" (Lynch 1960) existed. It follows, therefore, that perceptual/cognitive evaluations of shopping may fail if all respondents are not sufficiently familiar with the study area in question. Eventually, Downs obtained 202 completed returns and from pilot studies and a review of the literature he structured nine concepts which he believed were major independent features of retail differentiation. Each of the concepts was given four bipolar scales in the form of the semantic differential as described by Osgood, Suci and Tannenbaum (1957).

Downs had certainly adopted a useful technique for deriving responses from a large group of respondents since Osgood *et al* (1957, p.84) suggest that the semantic differential can be administered 'at fairly high speed' and consider that up to 400 items may be evaluated. They also consider the technique to have wide applicability and claim (1957, p.77) "there is no general semantic differential test as such ... it is the nature of the problem, then, that chiefly defines the class and form of the concept to be selected". Indeed, it has been widely and successfully applied by many researchers, for example, Sanoff and Sawhney (1970), Canter and Thorne (1972) and Craik (1968). In Down's study, each respondent was to evaluate all the bipolar scales along a seven-point scale from positive to negative aspects of the construct under question resulting in a 202 by 36 by 7 matrix of responses. The data were subjected to principal components analysis, correlating a 36 by 36 matrix. Downs had hypothesised that his nine major constructs should emerge as independent evaluative structures.

In the event, eleven components emerged, not all of which were easily decipherable and eventually, Downs was able to label and accept eight overall constructs for the evaluation of centres. Sarre (1972) has presented a valuable critique of the work of Downs, noting that the use of a bipolar adjectival technique has apparent limitations. Conceptually, Downs appeared to analyse individual perceptions of his study area, but produced group conclusions. The internal variance of a group response aggregated from individual concepts may tend to obliterate important results, argued Sarre. More importantly, Sarre suggested that Downs' basic concepts - upon which the respondents made their judgements - may possibly have been inappropriate and certainly his nine hypothesised constructs failed to emerge. Sarre suggested that the scales presented for analysis may have been too exogenously derived which:

"... leads one to doubt whether they can be genuinely representative of the importance of concepts actually in use" (by respondents/shoppers)."

though he is forced to admit that

"A particularly important feature of his method was the use of a standard form of response so that interrelationships could be analysed by statistical methods."

(Sarre 1972, p.32).

Sarre then proceeded to discuss unrestrained elicitation of mental models which should be free of external demands and constraints placed, perhaps falsely, by the interviewer. His deliberations led to a consideration of the work of Kelly (1955) and probably the earliest example relating this theory to retailing came in the work of Hudson (1974) who, in a wide-ranging analysis of spatial behaviour based on shopping diaries, made use of Kelly's Repertory Grid Technique. Crucially, his analysis focussed upon individual shops rather than groups of shops and Hudson invoked the problems encountered by Downs as one basis for this decision. In all, eleven shops (those most frequently used as evidenced by preliminary diary data) were analysed. Constructs "were drawn forth via the presentation of random triads of shops' names to each person." (Hudson, 1974 p.186). Hudson went on to ask each person to scale the shops on each of the constructs so elicited, on an eleven point scale.

Unlike Sarre, Hudson finds no problem in deriving generalisations from the opinions of individuals and the veracity of his arguments are accepted in this study. Hudson believes that it is possible to generalise about groups of people even where data are gathered at individual level. The problem becomes one of ensuring that if data are grouped this is done in such a way that important individual variations are not totally submerged. For example, eight persons, asked to analyse some stimulus on a scale from one to seven, may give a mean score of four. They may achieve this by all rating the stimulus as four, or by four rating the stimulus as seven and

44

four rating it as one. The mean score is the same in both
cases, but the responses by the individuals are quite different.
Evidently, Hudson believes such problems can be overcome.

Hudson's results revealed that indivduals offered between
seven and 17 constructs, with a median value of 11.5, this
from a final response group of 26. Hudson was able to attempt
principal components analysis of the constructs though of more
interest here is the range of constructs actually elicited.
Twenty-four constructs were mentioned by two or more persons
from the full list of 26 but only two were mentioned by all
respondents. It is useful to note that for students, who can
be characterised as a 'low income' group, the two constructs
mentioned by all of them were 'price' and 'location relative
to home'.

The essential point about Hudson's research is that it
presents a methodology for the objective elicitation of constructs that relate to shopping. This dismisses the criticism
that Sarre was able to make of Downs' earlier study. There is
no suggestion here that the constructs are supplied or suggested
by the researcher. Indeed, though the Kelly technique has
now been frequently applied in geographical research, it is
useful to delve a little further into its workings. Hudson's
confidence that his 'constructs' on shopping were objectively
derived stems from the use of Kelly's repertory grid which
does not permit the researcher to 'impose' ideas upon the
subject. Instead, the subject is placed into a situation
where an individually-held belief, yardstick or 'construct'
must be drawn upon to make a judgement between sets of alterna-
tives. The judgement that identifies the underlying construct
is elicited by offering the subject three stimuli and simply
suggesting that one of the three differs in some way from the
other two. The dimensions of that difference are not suggested
and the subject must draw upon his or her own experience in
order to express in what way any difference is perceived. The
major practical difficulty with this approach lies with its
extremely time-consuming nature and Hudson spent up to three
hours with an individual respondent during his research. This
was not a great problem for Hudson since he was dealing with
26 university undergraduates but there are several hundred
individuals living in the catchment area of ASDA Waterlooville
and Havant Hypermarket and direct application of Hudson's
methodology seemed impracticable.

Fortunately, as Fransella and Bannister (1977) have shown,
there are now numerous types of Kelly grid in use ranging from
a simple binary matrix to complex scaled matrices. Hudson
used a scaled matrix and its additional complexity made it

amenable to multivariate statistical analysis. It is clear that the Kelly technique can be time-consuming and in this respect Downs had a considerable advantage in using his semantic differential approach in which rapid completion by the respondents is a major feature. Fransella and Bannister (1977, p.40) outline a Kelly-type 'rating grid' which they see as 'similar to the semantic differential devised by Osgood and his colleagues' in that it has bipolar constructs and the respondent places a rating along the scale defined by the poles. Whereas the semantic differential supplies the constructs possibly at the whim of the researcher, this Kelly grid derives constructs by the repertory grid methodology, thereby minimising the input from the researcher. Once the constructs are identified, the rating grid should be as quick and as easy to use as the semantic differential and may be treated as such to be analysed by the familiar technique of principal components analysis. Such an approach was very attractive as a technique for comparing perceptual evaluations of Havant Hypermarket and Asda Waterlooville though many other perceptual approaches do exist. Indeed, note may be made at this stage of an alternative approach to retail evaluation followed by Spencer (1980). This makes use of the technique of multidimensional scaling, a wider consideration of which is offered by Brummell and Harman (1974). Interestingly, Spencer (1979) had considered the use of Personal Construct Theory but had rejected the idea on the grounds that it was time-consuming and that a consensus view was hard to obtain. Indeed, Spencer (1979) suggested that the orthogonal dimensions of the multidimensional space "might perhaps be regarded as bundles of personal constructs" (p.2). Spencer's survey of 381 housewives in Nelson and Colne, Lancashire, produced 200 multi-dimensional scales of seven shopping places (the stimuli) which ranged from the 'local shop' to a nearby ASDA store. Clearly there are lessons to be learned from this type of approach though the wider scale of inquiry, where the stimuli varied widely in nature, cannot be closely compared with the topic under study here.

One concern of Spencer that can be expanded upon was his desire for a less idiographic approach. A number of other researchers have followed the path of general modelling of individual behaviour. Cadwallader (1981) has proposed a 'cognitive gravity model', in part bridging the gap between modelling and behavioural approaches. Cadwallader's work in west Los Angeles with a sample of 53 households, focussed on shopper usage of competing supermarkets and shopping centres. Just four measures of attractiveness were derived for supermarkets and four different measures were used for shopping centres. The five supermarkets and shopping centres under

46

study were rated by the respondents on a seven-point scale. Three forms of regression model were used to predict shopper usage of the supermarkets and centres and the success rate was around 66 percent for supermarkets and 50 percent for shopping centres. This approach has the merit of combining some behavioural elements into a modelling approach and again follows the format of producing a generalised model from individual inputs.

Proponents of revealed space preference theory have increasingly turned to behavioural inputs for more sophisticated levels of explanation. Timmermans has been active in producing a wide range of models, including the conjoint measurement technique. A particular advantage of this approach is that genuine attention is paid to underlying attributes of the stimuli themselves; that is, the shops or shopping centres. It must be evident that the choice of the stimuli and their implied relationship and meaning for the respondents is crucial - and a source of potential weakness. Timmermans (1980a) illustrates the conjoint measurement approach in that he covers not just the common additive approaches, but also multiplicative, distributive, and dual-distributive aspects. Like the information integration approaches, the additive conjoint methodology is not unlike analysis of variance. The multiplicative form of the model, unlike the additive, assumes that some low overall score on a particular attribute will give an overall low score and cannot be compensated for by a higher evaluation of some other attribute. Timmermans goes on to present as stimuli 27 hypothetical shopping centres, with three attributes; number of shops, travel time and parking time. Supplied to 18 respondents, these stimuli allowed the testing of eight models. Unfortunately "the findings are rather inconclusive" (Timmermans 1980a, p.299), though at the aggregate level the multiplicative model seemed to be superior.

This suggests that, if we are to study constraints on behaviour, one single constraint may invalidate the use of an otherwise highly-regarded shopping opportunity. In the present case study it is certain that, for the poorer sectors of society, accessibility functions as just such a key constraint. In seeking to improve his models, Timmermans has presented further approaches. For example, Timmermans *et al* (1982a) actually adopt the Kelly repertory grid method to evaluate 13 existing shopping centres in Eindhoven. This is subsequent to applications of information integration (1981a), compositional multi-attribute evaluation models (1981b), and spatial choice models (1980b). Note that the centres presented as stimuli, though mostly of post-war construction, do have contrasting structural forms though the nucleated form dominates. Twenty respondents in the 1982 survey evaluated the 13 Eindhoven centres and between eight and 16 constructs per person emerged, with an average of 11.8 whilst 236 con structs in total emerged. Principal components analysis was attempted, the underlying dimensions of components were iden-tified leading Timmermans *et al* to conclude (1982a, p.10).

"The repertory grid methodology constitutes a potentially fruitful method of eliciting attributes which consumers use to differentiate between shopping centres".

More recently, this has been substantiated by Coshall (1985) with respect to individual comparison goods stores. Timmermans has also aimed to produce aggregate models with behavioural dimensions as independent variables. What this does not tell us, though it is hinted at by the multiplicative conjoint model, is whether or not some basic constraint will influence behaviour even though it does not influence preference. Such a point was at least implied in the work of Gayler (1980) in Vancouver. He disaggregated consumer groups by social class and related this to distance travelled to purchase a range of goods. For groceries, when distances are measured from home to shop, higher status groups are seen to make longer trips, by-passing supermarkets to shop at food halls in downtown department stores.

The foregoing studies show clearly that considerable progress is being made in the analysis of preferred* shopping locations. It is clear that such studies are a major challenge to aggre-gate, normative, predictive models that may best be seen as planning tools for use before new developments are finalised. The crushing challenge to the nearest centre hypothesis makes it evident that behavioural inputs must form a part of any comprehensive analysis of contemporary shopping patterns. Of crucial relevance here is that objective reality may be hard to define for all consumers within the catchment areas of very large stores. As will be seen below, reality is what people perceive it to be. A key approach to the analysis of what exactly constitutes satisfactory shopping opportunities — within a framework of welfare and social justice - may well best be determined by asking the customers themselves.

* Note the debate between MacLennan and Williams, Timmermans and Rushton (1979) on this possibly semantic point.

WELFARE TYPE APPROACHES

At this point one may abstract from the body of retail research such material as might be perceived as having a firmer basis in the welfare paradigm. This would then offer a clear spring-board into the present study and for this reason such work is treated separately. In reality, as expected, very little work in retail geography has been undertaken from an overtly welfare standpoint. Initially it must be determined whose 'welfare' has generally been under scrutiny in past studies, given that in the present work the focus is on the welfare of the consumer. It is evident that retail change of any form generates external-ities and much of the work to date has centred on how these affect rival traders – though this has long-run implications for the consumer and to that extent any 'impact' work has welfare implications. Guy (1976) and Thorpe *et al* (1976) try to show, either quantitatively or by means of other approaches, what the true effects of superstores is likely to be. Thorpe *et al* (1976) not only examine changes in shopper habits but consider retailer attitudes and conclude (1976, p. 28).

> "There is clearly no dramatic decline in the
> prosperity of the independent trader".

and, (1976, p.31)

> "The impact of superstores is not great on those
> parts of the retail structure which it might be
> desirable to bolster for social reasons".

Such a comment depends on one's definition of exactly which parts of the structure it is desirable to bolster. Thorpe clearly refers to the small shop sector while this study expresses some concern for the high street supermarket. What is clear is that the 'impact study' type of format, though most commonly seen as a 'modelling technique' and equally commonly concerned with the welfare of rival traders rather than of shoppers, does have relevance in the present context.

IMPACT STUDIES

An enthusiasm for impact studies was detected both in France and in Britain in the early 1970s as planners in particular sought to gain information on large new stores. The impact study can be a very quick and direct way of gaining information on the way in which a new outlet is carving out a trading area. One common problem, however, has lain with the interpretation of results since there was an inclination to attribute any store closure in the vicinity of a large new store directly to the 'impact' of that store without considering change in its widest sense. The balance of evidence has, with hindsight, moved away from blaming large new stores for all local retail change. The impact study, though direct, also tends to be both place-specific and time-specific and many are critical of the whole approach. It is, however, one that may be of use here since so many of the pitfalls are overcome by having such very comparable stores with which to work.

Another aspect of retail research with clear welfare implications is that by Kirby, Olsen, Sjoholt and Stolen (1981). Their study of shops in sparsely populated areas stemmed from a report in 1976 by a Norwegian Royal Commission. This had identified a loss of grocery stores averaging 217 outlets per annum (between 1963 and 1972). Between 1972 and 1975 there was a net loss of 383 outlets per annum. This had implications for the rural dispersed population and by 1975, 500 communities were 'shopless', being more than eight km from the nearest shop. Also, 1,300 stores were 'last shops' where the distance was more than four km to the next outlet. There were three major strategies adopted to reverse this trend, provided the 'last shop' fulfilled certain basic criteria. However, the present study area is far from the extremes of this Norwegian case study. Wilson (1981) and Coelho and Wilson (1976) have produced models that seek to maximise consumers' welfare, but these are rare applications of a welfare approach. Attitudes expressing concern over provision of specific types of shop do, of course, exist, as exemplified by the work of Kirby *et al* in Norway. Indeed, the whole field of small shop studies has a tendency toward protectionist attitudes, (see, for example, Davies and Kirby 1980 pp.173-75). Dawson (1983) makes useful distinctions between small shops and local shops and goes on to discuss policies that might assist independent retailers in their fight for survival. One such policy would be subsidies in cash or training. Another would be encouragement to small shops to join retail 'chains' and another would be to improve the transport system. Non-travel based solutions would include mobile shops or the information-based approach outlined by Davies and Champion (1980). Dawson outlines likely policy differences between urban and rural areas, a distinction that is useful in the present context, and notes:

"The more radical policy approaches all involve
the active collaboration of large retail
organisations with the public service sector."

(Dawson 1983, p.25)

Dawson's comment is an entirely appropriate point at which to look back and consider the techniques that were seen as fitting within an overarching framework of welfare, since policy prescriptions are an ultimate aim of this work. With regard to welfare, it was felt that the clearest path forward lay with 'subjective social indicators' as measured by powerful techniques that are able to pick up the subtleties of individual preference. For the population within the study area – the catchment areas of ASDA, Waterlooville and Havant Hypermarket – the most suitable technique appeared to be a Kelly repertory grid providing the constructs for a semantic differential. In this way, it should be possible to obtain a large sample of responses from residents living near ASDA, Waterlooville and Havant Hypermarket and thereby discover their perceptual evaluations of the two stores. The 'managers' of the urban system are far fewer in number and their opinions might best be obtained through unstructured interviews as outlined by Oppenheim (1966, pp 204-211) and Moser and Kalton (1971). Certainly, Helmstadter (1970, pp. 75-77) supports the value of the unstructured interview in dealing with the opinions of small numbers of people and, equally, outlines some of the pitfalls.

The comparison of the two stores themselves is ideal for an 'impact' approach since the two stores are within the same area and were opened at nearly the same time. It was seen as an opportunity to cast light on the true value of impact studies since no two stores have offered a more suitable background for impact analysis. Probably the most difficult aspect of the study came with the requirement to study the 'social' aspects of shopping and considerable detail will be needed on individuals and their attitude to shopping. Equally, those constrained in terms of their shopping must be identified and it is appropriate to measure this at the same time as 'social attitudes' since it is not possible to predict in advance which shoppers will be constrained and which will be free to exhibit preferences. Much reliance will have to be placed on dimensions already identified by Bruce (1974) and others, as being crucial to 'social' aspects of shopping and these will be set alongside criteria such as driving licence holding which are seen by Hillman (1976) as vital aspects of accessibility.

The following three chapters approach incrementally the issues of welfare and accessibility. Chapter four is devoted to an 'impact study' which provides the basic dimensions of store performance. Chapter five builds on this by offering a 'subjective social indicators' approach through a perceptual evaluation of the stores. Chapter six seeks to be more overtly welfare-related by disaggregating the catchment areas and characterising groups of shoppers as higher income or lower income. It is hoped that this dichotomisation will permit 'relative disadvantage' in respect of shopping to be revealed despite the fact that the study area in general is affluent.

51

4 Impact study of Asda Waterlooville and Havant Hypermarket

INTRODUCTION

If there genuinely is a welfare-related dimension to shopping then it should emerge at whatever scale of inquiry is attempted. It may well be that only relative disadvantage can be identified within this present, affluent, study area. That disadvantage, however, should be observable whether one is looking at the two stores, at their patrons or at specific sub-groups within the community. Accordingly, an approach was taken that sought to cumulate information on welfare. It started at the most general level and culminated with attention being paid to quite specific groups that were hypothesised to contrast in terms of welfare. At the widest, most 'macro', level was an analysis of the trading characteristics of the stores themselves. This drew upon an analysis of patrons at the two stores and could in theory involve the participation of residents from the whole of the wider study area. This 'impact study' was greatly facilitated by the fact that the two stores were so close both spatially and in opening dates. The impact study is outlined in detail in this chapter.

The approach taken in the impact study was to interview shoppers at each of the two stores as they left having made their purchases. The widest trading area of both stores was expected to cover all of the general study area and possibly beyond. It was hypothesised that within those trading areas, the stores would differ in terms of the types of individuals they would attract. In general welfare terms, the expectation was that the less mobile sectors of the community might be constrained to use the ASDA store while the more mobile groups could exercise choice. This simple hypothesis would founder if the stores proved to act as pure mutual intervening opportunities with all persons from the west of the area using ASDA and those from the east using Havant Hypermarket. This could be tested by dividing the general study area into more manageable units encompassing the major centres of population. Such 'home area' units would also be a useful basis for statistical analysis of the overall results and the 'home areas' finally decided upon, and numbered 1 to 19, are shown in Figure 4.1.

Although the need to discover the home area of an individual respondent was the key element of the interview scheduled devised for the 'impact study', attention should also be paid to the other factors deemed worthy of inclusion.

An adjunct question to the one on home location related to journey times to the store, since accessibility is of vital concern to this study. This is not a straightforward issue since Havant Hypermarket has very good motorway connections and some shoppers could travel a considerable distance to the store in a short space of time. What such a question should clarify is if one store has a marked ability to draw customers over a wider travel-time area. It cannot be assumed that all shoppers begin their journey at home and there are real grounds for expecting that ASDA shoppers in particular would have the opportunity to shop elsewhere (particularly in Waterlooville's 150 other shops) and this interacts with social aspects of shopping. The impact study thus had to allow for trips that started or ended other than at home and this may relate to mode of transport. Respondents at the two stores were expected to differ in their usage of various modes of transport with the car expected to dominate patterns at Havant Hypermarket. The car has been seen as a mobile shopping basket and since it is presumed that the more affluent will use Havant Hypermarket for expensive bulk purchases then another question had to relate to the amount of money spent on food.

Though patterns of retail change are not a central concern here, much attention in impact studies has been paid to the question of impact on other traders in the area - especially with reference to 'polarisation theory'. Accordingly, it was important to determine if it was supermarkets or corner shops that were most affected by the two stores and questions relating to this were included. The bulk of the questions so far devised have related to the use made of the two stores by their respective customers. Equally relevant to this study are the differ-

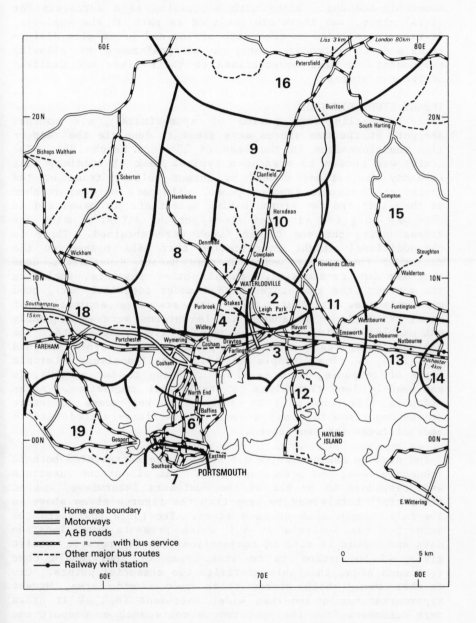

Figure 4.1   Boundaries of home areas of shoppers at ASDA,
Waterlooville, and Havant Hypermarket as used in 'impact study'

ences between those customers themselves. One vital area in which they were expected to contrast was in terms of car ownership and this, along with occupation as a surrogate for social class, was therefore included as part of the analysis. It was also decided to take note of sex and group size differences and to introduce concepts of preference by allowing respondents to make observations on their likes and dislikes of the two stores.

IMPACT STUDY FINDINGS
After a settling-down period of approximately six months, shoppers at the two stores were asked to complete the respective questionnaires in the week of 23 - 28 March 1981. The timing was chosen to present a typical week of trading, free from any distortions caused by summer holiday trade or the Easter or Christmas trading peaks. Shoppers were approached as they left the two stores having made their purchases and in this way only the views of those persons actually using the stores during the one trading week were obtained. There is the additional slight complication that ASDA opened on the Monday of the survey week, whereas Havant Hypermarket used that day for re-stocking. In all other respects, including the weather, the two stores traded under identical background circumstances. At ASDA, 1371 customers were approached of whom, 195 declined to answer and 16 returns were subsequently not usable, leaving a final sample of 1160 respondents. The equivalent figures for Havant Hypermarket were 1767, 433 and 22, giving a final sample of 1312 questionnaires. Certain types of response, such as those relating to car parking, do not readily lend themselves to statistical comparison. Attention is therefore paid to just eight key areas of store cross-comparison that may reveal real welfare-related differences between the two stores.

The data in tables 4.1 to 4.8 inclusive are presented both in frequency count and percentage form. Not all of the questions were responded to by all of the customers interviewed and so the overall totals may be less than the figures given above as the full sample size at each store. The table that sets the scene for the analysis is 4.1 which presents home location data and should be read in conjunction with Figure 4.1. Whilst giving no indication as to what types of individuals come from each area, the table clarifies two essential points. One is that though both stores trade over a wide area, Havant Hypermarket has a somewhat wider catchment in that it draws more customers from the most remote zones such as Gosport and Petersfield. This follows from the fact that it is a larger store and more accessible to motorway traffic. When the nearer areas are studied it becomes clear that there is an extent to

Table 4.1
Frequency distribution of customer origins (home areas) of patrons using ASDA, Waterlooville, and Havant Hypermarket

Home area — Numbers of shoppers coming from each home area to respective stores

Home area	Havant Hypermarket Number of respondents	Percentage of respondents	ASDA, Waterlooville Number of respondents	Percentage of respondents
Southsea	27	(2.1)	17	(1.5)
Portsmouth	73	(5.6)	21	(1.8)
Cosham	91	(6.9)	44	(3.8)
Southborne	19	(1.4)	6	(0.5)
Chichester	36	(2.7)	5	(0.4)
Funtington	3	(0.2)	3	(0.3)
Clanfield	16	(1.2)	25	(2.2)
Swanmore	14	(1.1)	19	(1.6)
Denmead	18	(1.4)	79	(6.8)
Fareham	38	(2.9)	13	(1.1)
Purbrook	101	(7.7)	146	(12.6)
Leigh Park	177	(13.5)	23	(2.0)
Horndean	94	(7.2)	309	(26.6)
Hayling Island	73	(5.6)	12	(1.0)
Emsworth	83	(6.3)	11	(0.9)
Waterlooville	102	(7.8)	346	(30.0)
Gosport	11	(0.8)	2	(0.2)
Out of area	47	(3.6)	29	(2.5)
Petersfield	47	(3.7)	18	(1.5)
Havant	48	(18.4)	32	(2.7)
	1312	(99.9)	1160	(100.0)

TOTALS

χ^2 Analysis: Calculated χ^2 = 748.59, df = 19, p < 0.05

which the stores function as intervening opportunities since, for example, Denmead residents tend to use ASDA whereas Chichester residents use Havant Hypermarket.

This situation is precisely what might have been anticipated and shows that the two stores are in general competition for the bulk purchase market, but that there is clear scope for individual choice and preference. The catchment areas are very broadly defined in order to cope with the mass of data, but there is some evidence that in the 'zone of indifference' (Purbrook and Waterlooville) ASDA tends to dominate.

Further aspects of Table 4.1 that are noteworthy include the phenomenon of Leigh Park for whose residents Havant Hypermarket was by far the preferred destination. Many residents of the extreme western edge of the large Leigh Park estate probably found Havant Hypermarket to be accessible on foot. For persons constrained to shop on foot ASDA would not have been a viable alternative. Note that residents from Denmead and Hambledon, the areas that lay in relation to ASDA as Leigh Park did to Havant Hypermarket, did not so overwhelmingly support ASDA. Denmead is a more affluent area and its residents could probably exercise greater choice in terms of food store patronised. There was a tendency for ASDA to dominate the west and draw especially heavily upon Waterlooville. Havant Hypermarket dominated the east and the outlying areas but generally 'creamed off trade all round' in the classic hypermarket manner. As confirmation that the stores did differ in respect of catchment areas the visual evidence was supplemented by statistical analysis. This showed a highly significant difference between the stores in this respect (χ^2 = 748.59, df = 19, p < 0.05).

WELFARE ASPECTS
The first table from which direct information on welfare aspects may be drawn is Table 4.2. It has been suggested by Hillman and others that shopping is undertaken on trips where other errands are also done and thus stores in established centres are to be preferred. It should be the case, then, that ASDA has a greater percentage of individuals either beginning or ending their journeys at some location other than home. Table 4.2 shows that whilst both stores are dominated by trips that both commence and terminate at home, ASDA has slightly fewer such trips. There is very little difference in the two stores as regards trips that end at home but did not commence there and this covers the situation where the shopper takes in a visit to a foodstore on the way home perhaps from work. ASDA has markedly more people who have come from home but are not directly returning there and people who have neither come from home nor are returning there. The general feeling is that

Table 4.2
Frequency distribution of total trips made to ASDA, Waterlooville, or Havant Hypermarket by origin and destination.

Trip Type	Store			
	Havant Hypermarket		ASDA, Waterlooville	
	Number of respondents	Percentage of respondents	Number of respondents	Percentage of respondents
1. Total where trip begins at home; ends at home	853	(65.4)	602	(51.9)
2. Total where trip begins at home; does not end at home	113	(8.7)	201	(17.3)
3. Total where trip does not begin at home; ends at home	288	(22.1)	278	(23.9)
4. Total where trip neither begins nor ends at home	50	(3.8)	79	(6.8)
TOTALS	1304	(100.0)	1160	(99.9)

χ^2 Analysis: Calculated χ^2 = 66.47, df = 3, p < 0.05

59

ASDA interacts more with other destinations though, inevitably, both stores are dominated by one-stop-shopping. This reflects the sheer bulk of purchases which usually demands that they be returned home directly - especially if frozen products are purchased.

Table 4.2 was statistically analysed and this again confirmed that the stores differ (χ^2 = 66.74, df = 3, p < 0.05). Journey times are presented in Table 4.3 and here the welfare implications are harder to discern. The location of Havant Hypermarket near a motorway interchange meant that far wider areas were accessible in, say, 5 minutes, than would be the case at ASDA Waterlooville. It was clear that Havant Hypermarket was generating more longdistance trips but also dominating in the 'under 5 minute' category and both reflect its motorway orientation. ASDA shopping tended to peak in the '5 - 9 minutes' and '10 - 14 minutes' categories which may have indicated the difficulties in reaching a district centre. The test statistic is again significant (χ^2 = 25.91, df = 5, p < 0.05) but the data would need to be more thoroughly unravelled and weighting made for accessibility before welfare implications could be read into this.

Welfare issues were far more to the fore in Table 4.4 showing mode of transport used to reach the stores. As predicted for this generally affluent area, car-borne shoppers dominate. The car is totally dominant at Havant Hypermarket with 89.7 percent of shoppers sampled having arrived by car - a far higher percentage than at ASDA. The car seems to be almost essential for hypermarket shoppers though, as already noted, some residents of nearby Leigh Park can reach the store on foot and examination of the returns showed that Leigh Park residents did indeed dominate this latter category. The most interesting categories are the ones that show more than twice as many ASDA shoppers arriving on foot and almost six times as many arriving by bus. For groups constrained to use such modes of transport the clear implication is that ASDA is more accessible. When mode of transport was related to length of journey, it emerged that the longer trips to both stores (more than 20 minutes) often involved customers who came by bus or on foot. For example, the most typical journey time by bus to ASDA was in the 20 to 30 minute category and this exemplifies the real problems faced by those who lack a car. When Table 4.4 was statistically analysed the results confirmed a great deal of difference between the stores (χ^2 = 185.64, df = 4, p < 0.05) and provide a clear evidence of a welfare dimension since the less mobile tend to use ASDA.

60

Table 4.3
Frequency distribution of time taken by shoppers to reach
ASDA, Waterlooville, and Havant Hypermarket

Duration of Journey	Totals in each category at:			
	Havant Hypermarket		ASDA, Waterlooville	
	Number of respondents	Percentage of respondents	Number of respondents	Percentage of respondents
Under 5 minutes	275	(21.0)	215	(18.5)
5 to 9 minutes	253	(19.3)	320	(27.6)
10 to 14 minutes	388	(29.6)	318	(27.4)
15 to 19 minutes	178	(13.6)	132	(11.4)
20 to 30 minutes	167	(12.7)	143	(12.3)
Over 30 minutes	51	(3.9)	32	(2.7)
TOTALS	1312	(100.1)	1160	(99.9)

χ^2 Analysis: Calculated χ^2 = 25.91, df = 5, p < 0.05

Table 4.4
Frequency distribution of mode of transport used by patrons visiting ASDA, Waterlooville, and Havant Hypermarket

Mode of Transport	Totals in each category at:			
	Havant Hypermarket		ASDA, Waterlooville	
	Number of respondents	Percentage of respondents	Number of respondents	Percentage of respondents
Foot	90	(6.9)	187	(16.1)
Cycle	10	(0.8)	5	(0.4)
Motorcycle	9	(0.7)	10	(0.9)
Bus	26	(2.0)	152	(13.1)
Car	1177	(89.7)	806	(69.5)
TOTALS	1312	(100.1)	1160	(100.0)

χ^2 Analysis: Calculated χ^2 = 185.64, df = 4, p < 0.05

It has often been noted that shopping trips may be deferred until the family car is available and such a possibility is facilitated by the long opening hours of the two stores. In other words, the simple analysis of mode of transport to the stores may blur real differences in background characteristics of those who use them. In some ways a more adequate welfare measure is to examine the actual car ownership patterns of those who choose to use the two stores. The clear picture to emerge from Table 4.5 is that both stores attract shoppers from households with a car. Households lacking a car, where the clearest welfare problems might be found, are overwhelmed by the numbers of households with one car and even two. Indeed, at Havant Hypermarket, as many households had three or more cars as had none. It must be borne in mind that this is an affluent part of the country with high levels of car ownership, further emphasising that it is relative, not absolute, disadvantage that will be found. Even so, the two stores differ markedly in terms of the car-ownership patterns of their clientele. Only 7.9 percent of respondents at Havant Hypermarket came from households lacking a car and the bulk of these were drawn from the nearby fringes of Leigh Park where 33 percent of respondents stated that their household had no car. Overall, ASDA attracts nearly twice as many customers from households with no car and this is a crucial accessibility factor. Such clear differences gain the expected confirmation from statistical analysis (χ^2 = 54.64, df = 3, p < 0.05) showing measurable differences in levels of car ownership between patrons of the two stores.

As Chapter 2 postulated, accessibility is perhaps the key dimension of a spatial analysis of welfare and the tables covered thus far have all elaborated upon that dimension. Overwhelmingly, ASDA and Havant Hypermarket do contrast on all the accessibility measures and this confirms that welfare factors can emerge even when a sample is taken of respondents from all parts of the study area. A picture is emerging of the ways in which individuals use the two stores with Havant Hypermarket attracting the more mobile consumer. At this point other tables can be used to flesh out the picture. The more mobile hypermarket user is probably also a freezer owner who might shop less frequently and spend more money per trip. Table 4.6 goes some way towards substantiating this (χ^2 = 111.81, df = 5, p < 0.05) by showing how ASDA shoppers dominate in the three categories of more frequent shopping and Havant Hypermarket shoppers in the three categories of less frequent shopping.

Table 4.5
Frequency distribution of number of cars in the
households from which store patrons are drawn

Number of cars in household	Totals in each category at:			
	Havant Hypermarket		ASDA, Waterlooville	
	Number of respondents	Percentage of respondents	Number of respondents	Percentage of respondents
None	103	(7.9)	173	(15.2)
One	784	(57.4)	682	(60.0)
Two	350	(26.9)	238	(20.9)
Three or more	103	(7.9)	44	(3.9)
TOTALS	1340	(100.1)	1137	(100.0)

χ^2 Analysis: Calculated χ^2 = 54.64, df = 3, p < 0.05

Table 4.6
Frequency distribution of frequency with which patrons visit chosen store

Frequency of visits	Havant Hypermarket		ASDA, Waterlooville	
	Number of respondents	Percentage of respondents	Number of respondents	Percentage of respondents
Three times a week or more	65	(5.3)	127	(11.3)
Twice a week	121	(9.8)	195	(17.4)
Once a week	583	(47.2)	563	(50.3)
Once a fortnight	191	(15.4)	104	(9.3)
Once a month	153	(12.4)	81	(7.2)
Less often	123	(10.0)	49	(4.4)
TOTALS	1236	(100.1)	1119	(99.9)

χ^2 Analysis: Calculated χ^2 = 111.81, df = 5, p < 0.05

One frequent concern in retailing studies is to gain some
measure of 'social class' of the respondents. Invariably this
requires the use of some surrogate measure and it is fortunately possible to estimate social class from occupational
data. The registrar – general utilises tables which permit
every occupation to be used as the basis for allocating individuals either to Social Classes or to Socio-economic groups.
It was decided that this procedure should be adopted and, from
knowledge of actual occupation, respondents could be ascribed
to the standard Social Classes (I, II, III(N), III(N), IV or
V). Ultimately, to facilitate comparison with other works in
retailing, the Classes were redefined as A, B, C1, C2, D, E
which is the more familiar form. Social class can be seen as
a surrogate for measures of wealth that would be far more
difficult to obtain. Likewise, it was demonstrated in Chapter
3 that 'social class' has frequently been shown to be a key
determinant of shopping behaviour. The figures for social
class of respondents at the two stores based on the surrogate
of occupation can be seen in Table 4.7. It is clear that Havant
Hypermarket has markedly more A and B group respondents and
markedly fewer D and E group respondents. Since the higher
status groups will be more mobile it follows that those most
able to exercise choice are more frequently represented at
Havant Hypermarket. The corollary holds true – those most
likely to be constrained in their choice of shopping location
are most frequently found at ASDA. The differences demonstrated
in Table 4.7 are sufficiently marked that they can be confirmed
by statistical testing (χ^2 = 31.84, df = 5, p < 0.05).

The pattern of the estimated age of shoppers at the two stores
is shown in Table 4.8. It serves as a useful counterpoint to
the welfare variables thus far analysed. Whilst there are
good theoretical reasons to expect differences between the
stores on accessibility grounds, there is no reason to expect
that they will attract shoppers from different age groups.
That said, there is a slight relationship between age and
social status. Nevertheless, it would be disturbing if the
two stores showed marked differences on this dimension since
it might imply that they are competing for completely different
sectors of the market. Examination of Table 4.8 shows this
not to be the case and this is confirmed statistically (χ^2 =
12.42, df = 4, p > 0.05) revealing no significant difference.
Havant Hypermarket dominates most clearly in the age group 45-60
whilst ASDA has noticeably more 25-34 year old shoppers but
overall, the stores are similar. This table lends added weight
to the earlier findings where expected differences did emerge.
It would be too difficult to attempt a table showing how the
two stores contrast in terms of the many stores from which
they divert trade. However, only 0.5 per cent of stores exper-

66

Table 4.7
Frequency distribution of estimate of social class of
respondents at each store, based on stated occupation
of the head of the household

Social class groupings	Totals in each category at:			
	Havant Hypermarket		ASDA, Waterlooville	
	Number of respondents	Percentage of respondents	Number of respondents	Percentage of respondents
A	37	(2.8)	12	(1.0)
B	189	(14.4)	126	(10.9)
C_1	442	(33.7)	378	(32.6)
C^2	338	(29.6)	377	(32.5)
D	206	(15.7)	182	(15.7)
E	50	(3.8)	85	(7.3)
TOTALS	1262	(100.0)	1160	(100.0)

χ^2 Analysis: Calculated χ^2 = 31.84, df = 5, p < 0.05

Table 4.8
Frequency distribution of estimated age of shoppers
at ASDA, Waterlooville, and Havant Hypermarket

Age group category	Totals in each category at:			
	Havant Hypermarket		ASDA, Waterlooville	
	Number of respondents	Percentage of respondents	Number of respondents	Percentage of respondents
Up to 25	57	(4.4)	47	(4.1)
25-34	274	(21.0)	289	(24.9)
35-44	381	(29.0)	353	(30.4)
45-60	400	(30.6)	287	(24.7)
Over 60	199	(15.1)	184	(15.9)
TOTALS	1311	(100.1)	1160	(100.0)

χ^2 Analysis: Calculated χ^2 = 12.42, df = 4, p > 0.05

68

iencing loss to Havant Hypermarket were identified as small or local shops and the figure is exactly the same for ASDA. On the other hand, ASDA most affected the Tesco supermarket at Waterlooville, followed by the Waitrose supermarket at Cowplain. Havant Hypermarket most affected the Tesco superstore in Portsmouth, followed by the Waitrose supermarket at Havant. This tends to lend support to 'polarisation theory', whereby superstores and hypermarkets divert trade from supermarkets, but co-exist with small shops.

SHOPPER OPINIONS
Attention is finally paid to the crucial question of what the respondents chose to mention when asked for their likes and dislikes about the stores. It is essential to note that no prompting of answers was made and the question was asked 'Do you have any likes or dislikes about this store?' This left open to the respondent the choice of topic and some respondents had no opinions, others offered many. One point that is worthy of note is that the interviews were on the store premises and attention was therefore focussed on what might be termed the physical aspects of the store. Very few respondents made reference to locational aspects of either store, preferring to concentrate on such factors as the price or quality of goods. Because the question was totally unconstrained, an extremely long and often idiosyncratic list of likes and dislikes emerged, with the former dominating. The full list of likes and dislikes obtained from customers at the two stores is shown in Tables 4.9 and 4.10. These were seen as likely to provide valuable information on which to build a perceptual analysis of the stores since the comments were unconstrained and directly relevant to the stores.

Examination of the likes and dislikes shows the responses to be generally those that one might have expected - with the exception of the emphasis on dislike of trolleys. In the case of Havant Hypermarket these are stored out of doors and are consequently often wet. In the case of ASDA Waterlooville, the chosen trolley is left at the checkout and goods placed into the trolley vacated by the previous customer. This infuriates many who shop with small children as they cannot be sure the previous shopper will have used a trolley with a baby seat.

In the case of ASDA, the 'likes' are dominated by price, a factor that this store chain emphasises, whereas factors relating to convenience of shopping are more favoured at Havant Hypermarket. Nevertheless, if the top ten items at ASDA are correlated with the ranking of those same items at Havant Hypermarket, the results are highly significant (rs = +0.83, p < 0.01). There is thus further evidence that the stores

Table 4.9
Major aspects of ASDA, Waterlooville, mentioned by
shoppers as being a specific like or dislike

Total number of times this aspect mentioned as being liked	Aspect	Total number of times this aspect mentioned as being disliked
366	Prices	27
345	Internal layout	52
279	Under one roof	
192	Range or choice	58
182	Convenient location	3
159	Ease of parking	23
144	Cleanliness	
135	Size or spaciousness	38
111	Staff and services	18
104	Goods easy to find	43

Table 4.10
Major aspects of Havant, Hypermarket, mentioned by shoppers as being a specific like or dislike

Total number of times this aspect mentioned as being liked	Aspect	Total number of times this aspect mentioned as being disliked
570	Internal layout	45
459	All under one roof	2
277	Range or choice	63
262	Prices	33
242	Easy parking	4
213	Staff helpful	14
201	Conveniently located	10
151	Cleanliness/hygiene	
133	Restaurant	13
90	Size	13

are genuinely comparable, but that ASDA is more favourably
viewed in respect of the welfare-related item, price.

CONCLUSIONS
The results are thus encouraging and suggest that there are,
indeed, welfare-related differences between the stores. The
crucial facts are that ASDA attracts fewer people who arrived
by car and, more importantly since people may have parked
elsewhere, more people from households with no car. There was
also a higher percentage of 'E' social group respondents and
all of this indicates that ASDA is better placed to serve the
less advantaged groups. When likes and dislikes were elicited,
the most frequently mentioned factor at ASDA was price, already
noted as a vital welfare item. Even though store location was
not frequently mentioned, ASDA still gained a better evaluation
on this criterion. There is reason then, to suspect that the
following chapter, which concentrates upon a perceptual analysis of the two stores, will further illuminate welfare-related
differences especially with respect to measures of accessibility.

5 Perceptual evaluation of Asda Waterlooville and Havant Hypermarket

INTRODUCTION

In chapter two, consideration was given to the issue of disadvantage, both 'absolute' and 'relative', concluding that an
approach using 'subjective social indicators' would be most
likely to produce meaningful measures of these key concepts.
It was noted that Smith (1978 p.15) had stated:

> 'The social indicators approach emphasises that
> it is the way that individuals feel about things
> that really matters'.

From this it could be deduced that some estimate must be made
of the perceptions of hypermarkets and superstores as held by
the population at large. An important part of any welfare
approach should be to examine whether real differences
exist between consumers' evaluations of hypermarkets and superstores. It is to this issue that the present chapter addresses
itself through interviews with the shopping public at large.
This offers a more representative viewpoint than that gained
from those individuals already known to be using such stores
and whose opinions were sought in the research described in
the last chapter.

PERCEPTUAL ANALYSIS OF SHOPPING

It was demonstrated in chapter three that the use of Kelly's repertory grid methodology was the most reliable method for producing subjective constructs for a semantic differential scale. The use of this technique ensures that evaluations are based on constructs that are not devised or imposed by the interviewer. Subsequently, the use of semantic differential scales rather than repertory grids allows a wide range of individuals to be approached for their opinions – this is rather more difficult if the Kelly technique alone is used. Hudson (1974), relying on the views of a small sample of respondents, had found the interviews involving the Kelly technique could last several hours. Such a lengthy interview process might make it impossible to conduct such interviews with a large sample of individuals. Chapter three demonstrated that to use the Kelly technique with a small sample followed by the semantic differential with a larger sample was the ideal compromise. It would thereby be possible to show whether welfare considerations both of accessiblity and price were important factors in the shopping decision process of the general public. Nonetheless, it was recognised that it would still be necessary to find a small number of respondents who would be prepared to complete the intensive repertory grid interview process.

The latter subjects were identified in an earlier shopping study in the region (Hallsworth 1982) during which thirty-three individuals stated that they were prepared to be interviewed in respect of their shopping habits. These thirty-three individuals agreed to participate in a Kelly-type repertory grid analysis, and were interviewed in their homes. The majority were women (27 out of 33) and most lived throughout the wider study region (Figure 1.1). Respondents came dominantly from Portsmouth but interviews also took place in Gosport, Waterlooville, Cosham, Leigh Park and Cowplain.

CHOICE OF STIMULI FOR THE KELLY ANALYSIS

A crucial decision concerned the way in which stimuli should be used in order to elicit responses. No procedure is ever totally free of bias but, since the object was to discover the bases of discrimination used by consumers when choosing between grocery stores, photographs of such stores were chosen. Specifically, a postcard-sized black and white photograph was taken of every large grocery store in the study region – 38 in all. A standard procedure was adopted whereby the main frontage was photographed from across the street although in the case of the largest stores this was sometimes difficult. The objective was to ensure that the respondent could quickly identify a specific store. Should the individual be uncertain as to the

74

identity of a particular store, a prompt was available since the name of the store was written on the reverse of the photograph.

THE REPERTORY GRID ANALYSIS
At interview, the respondents were given all 38 photographs and asked to divide them into those stores which were either used and/or recognised, and those stores with which the individual was not familiar. Respondents were told that the address of the store was printed on the back of the photograph, but few needed to make this check. The repertory grid evaluation was based only on the photographs of the stores that were known by the respondents. The procedure was the customary one of 'triads' where respondents were offered sets of three randomly-selected photographs.

With each new presentation the question was asked: "In what way, if any, does one of these stores differ from the other two?" The process was repeated with new combinations of photographs until no new constructs emerged. This process took from 45 minutes to three hours. Table 5.1 summarises the range of constructs elicited from the 33 respondents. It is clear that some respondents have very complex evaluative criteria and one person produced 28 constructs. The median number of constructs produced was 14 whilst at the lower extreme one individual could supply only four constructs.

CONSTRUCTS DERIVED FROM THE REPERTORY GRID ANALYSIS
It had therefore proved possible to gain insights into the constructs used by individuals without in any way imposing the views or opinions of the interviewer. Table 5.1, which lists all items mentioned ten times or more, is a rich source of information that is of interest in its own right even though the prime aim was simply to identify the constructs on which grocery stores are evaluated. The most frequently mentioned construct is price, which is itself an important welfare-related variable. It was followed by parking, a construct related to accessibility and reflecting the above-average levels of car ownership in this area of the country. Twenty respondents mentioned convenience of location which neatly encapsulates the welfare concept. Nearness to other shops or facilities is another welfare-related factor that appears high on the list having been mentioned by 13 respondents, immediately followed by two other constructs with a locational dimension. In all, 76 constructs emerged, some being extremely idiosyncratic.

Table 5.1 Personal constructs relating to shopping as derived from a sample of 33 individuals living in South-East Hampshire

Respondent Number

Total number of times each construct mentioned MIN = 10	33	32	31	30	29	28	27	26	25	24	23	22	21	20	19	18	17	16	15	14	13	12	11	10	9	8	7	6	5	4	3	2	1	Construct Name
29	*	*	*				*	*	*	*	*	*	*	*	*	*	*	*	*	*	*	*	*	*	*	*	*	*	*	*	*	*	*	Pricing
24	*	*	*				*	*	*	*	*	*	*	*	*	*	*	*	*	*	*	*	*	*	*	*	*	*	*	*	*	*	*	Parking
24			*	*	*	*	*	*	*	*	*	*	*	*	*	*	*				*	*	*	*	*	*	*	*	*	*	*	*	*	Range/Variety
21		*		*			*	*	*	*	*		*	*	*	*	*	*	*		*	*	*	*	*	*		*	*	*	*	*	*	Checkouts and Queues
20	*	*		*	*	*	*	*	*	*		*	*	*	*	*	*	*	*	*	*	*	*	*	*	*	*	*	*	*	*	*	*	Size/Spaciousness
20	*	*		*	*	*	*	*	*	*	*	*	*	*	*		*			*	*	*	*	*	*	*	*	*	*	*	*	*	*	Internal layout (Especially Aisles)
20			*	*		*	*	*	*	*	*	*	*	*	*	*	*	*	*		*	*	*	*	*	*	*	*	*	*	*	*	*	Convenience of location
17	*			*	*	*		*	*	*				*	*	*	*	*			*		*	*			*	*		*	*	*	*	Quality
17		*	*	*	*	*	*	*	*	*	*		*	*	*	*	*	*			*	*	*			*	*	*	*	*	*	*	*	Cleanliness
15		*		*	*	*		*	*	*	*		*			*	*	*	*		*						*	*	*	*	*			Crowdedness
13			*	*	*				*	*	*	*	*	*	*	*	*	*		*	*	*		*			*	*	*	*	*	*	*	Nearness to Other Shops or Facilities
11		*				*	*	*						*		*		*			*		*	*					*			*	*	Near Work of Self or Partner
11	*				*	*	*		*				*	*	*		*	*		*	*	*	*	*	*	*	*	*		*			*	Used Only if in Area

76

The list of constructs is markedly more general and objective than the list of shopper likes and dislikes identified at ASDA and Havant Hypermarket. By taking the key elements from the full list of 76, it was possible to identify 30 variables representing a wide range of evaluative critera which could be presented to a wider sample of respondents in the specific study area (Figure 1.2). By casting these criteria as a series of semantic differential scales it would be possible to gain a large number of responses in no more time than the exhaustive repertory grid analysis had taken.

THE SEMANTIC DIFFERENTIAL TEST

In order to allow for a wide range of responses, use of the commonly used seven point semantic scale was adopted. The range of topics included the major evaluative criteria produced by the repertory grid analysis. After extensive piloting of the questionnaire, an earlier draft was amended to exclude reference to the restaurants at the two stores. It was decided to include, instead, the availability of boxes for carrying goods away. The reason for this was that the majority of people interviewed in the pilot studies lived so close to the stores that few of them bothered to use the restaurants. Since many large grocery stores still do not have a restaurant facility, this served to increase the possibility that this semantic scale might be used in a wide range of situations.

The 30 items on the semantic scale were representative of the views of the public and welfare factors such as price and nearness to other shops featured prominently. It was also felt that the other variables which emerged would be of value in terms of measuring relative disadvantage. Because this is a generally affluent area many shoppers are able to exercise choice and travel substantial distances to 'preferred' grocery stores. It was essential to give full prominence to more subjective factors that would attract the wealthy and mobile as well as the disadvantaged. A scale with 30 items was felt to be of sufficient complexity to give variety without being so long that individuals would be dissuaded from completing it. It was anticipated that several hundred individuals might be presented with the scale, thereby giving a wide representation of local shopper opinions.

STUDY AREA

Since the two stores have a capacity to attract shoppers from beyond the area mapped in Figure 1.1, it would have been reasonable to have administered the questionnaire anywhere in the general study region. The strongest perceptions, however, would come from those individuals for whom the two stores had become the nearest large-scale shopping opportunities. This factor focussed attention upon the area lying half way between the two stores. Within this area it was anticipated that most people would have considered using either ASDA or Havant Hypermarket. They would probably have made judgements based upon the factors listed on the 30-point scale and some would have begun to use the new stores. Others would have found that their existing grocery outlet continued to be preferable for them. The essence of the analysis was to discover if, when making judgements between stores, individuals regarded welfare-related issues as important. If such issues were important, it would next be possible to discover which store, ASDA or Havant Hypermarket, fared best in that respect. It was decided that a sample of 300 households would be both representative and manageable within the time constraints faced. A line of equidistance between the two stores was drawn and a full census was made of the 300 households lying closest to it. After multiple repeat visits, 260 households finally responded. The locations of the households and the grocery stores they state they were using were recorded. It emerged that ASDA and Havant Hypermarket had become important stores for shoppers in this area, but other stores still had their loyal customers.

CONDUCT OF INTERVIEWS
Data gathering was a simple procedure whereby individuals who had been identified as the person responsible for shopping for the household were invited to complete the questionnaire on their doorstep. They were urged to place ticks quickly and not to ponder the answers. The only other instruction was that they should place a tick on every line and that the stronger their opinion, the nearer the tick should be to the appropriate pole of the scale. It was found that responses could be obtained in as little as three minutes using this procedure. The opportunity was then taken to record respondents' present main grocery store and to note any observations they made on grocery shopping.

RESULTS FROM THE SEMANTIC DIFFERENTIAL TEST
The survey produced a total of 15,600 evaluations, half relating to ASDA and half to Havant Hypermarket. This was to be the basis for addressing the two key hypotheses relating to welfare. The first hypothesis sought to discover if welfare factors were important to individuals when they came to discriminate between stores. The second hypothesis was that if welfare matters were important, then ASDA should gain better evaluations than Havant Hypermarket.

It was necessary to produce from the aggregated information an overall 'group evaluation' by use of a technique for parsimonious data reduction. In this way, a clearer picture would emerge of which variables were truly important in respect of choosing between stores. Numerous techniques are available but, as shown in Chapter three, the semantic differential format was specifically devised for use with principal components analysis. In this case there was the expectation that welfare factors should form a dimension quite separate from the other elements on the scales. Not only was it necessary to reduce the data to more manageable proportions but it was also crucial to discover the underlying structure of the data. Specifically, the data had to be broken down into major subgroupings of factors that the respondents perceived as having much in common.

IDENTIFICATION OF SUB-GROUPS OF FACTORS
Within the broad family of Factor Analysis models the procedure of varimax rotation of the initial factor solution seemed to offer a technique that would achieve the desired objective of identifying sub-groups of variables. By rotating the initial factor solution, varimax specifically picks out the sub-groups of variables which have most in common in terms of their factor structure whilst, at the same time, retaining orthogonality in the data. In one procedure, therefore, the data could be both reduced and grouped into batches of variables showing greatest communality. It was decided to use this technique to analyse separately the ASDA responses and the Havant Hypermarket responses to see if both demonstrated a similar factorial pattern. That said, it was recognised that there were five measures that related welfare to accessibility and one, price, that tended to stand alone. This latter variable might be read in common with the accessibility factors or might vary, instead, with respect to other measures of store performance.

RESULTS OF THE GROUPING PROCEDURE
Table 5.2 shows the pattern that emerged when data on ASDA, Waterlooville, were subjected to principal components analysis with varimax rotation. For maximum clarity, only the highest loading of each individual variable has been included. It is common practise to exclude loadings lower than 0.5 and loadings lower than this are included only when they are the highest for a particular variable. The presentation chosen serves primarily to show the strongest associations of all the variables under consideration. The results are given in the same order that the questions were presented to the respondents and the actual order of emergence of the factors is noted.

Table 5.2
Five varimax-rotated principal components of the perceptual variables - ASDA, Waterlooville.

Stimuli from semantic scale (in order of presentation)	Loadings on the five components (in order of emergence)				
	4	1	2	5	3
Very conveniently located	.55				
Often visit other shops on same trip	.72				
Near a family workplace	.50				
In area I often visit	.77				
Good bus links	.45				
A store chain I like		.57			
Prices always low		.72			
Wide range or choice		.75			
Food always fresh		.70			
Good quality items		.70			
Good own-brand range		.63			
Good value overall		.72			
Everything available under one roof		.53			
Goods easy to find		.46			
Staff and services helpful			.45		
Excellent bakery				.51	
Good place to buy fish			.58		
Lack of boxes not a problem				.48	
Easy parking					.55
Good trolley system					.60
Few checkout queues			.56		
Good cheque and credit system					.72
Convenient opening hours					.47
Never blocked by shelf-filling			.68		
Internal layout excellent			.38		
Right size of store					.54
Always clean and hygienic				.60	
Never too crowded or congested			.58		
Friendly atmosphere			.48		
Store temperature just right					.44

It is immediately clear that the first hypothesis is confirmed in that the accessibility measures emerge together.
The respondents were clearly perceiving accessibility as a
unique dimension of store evaluation. Furthermore, price,
the other welfare factor, emerged separately from the accessibility measures. It grouped instead with a number of variables
that emphasised characteristics that would be important to
an individual once he or she had reached a selected store. It
was not surprising that price should emerge in the same component as 'good value overall'. Parking, a further factor of
relevance once the store had been reached, was associated with
another group of variables emerging as component three.

Attention was then turned to Havant Hypermarket and the
results obtained are presented in similar fashion in Table 5.3.
For the first two components there is a quite remarkable similarity in pattern. The first 14 variables emerge in association with the same pattern of components as had been the case
with ASDA. Accessibility factors were again separate from
other constructs and in this case all loadings exceeded 0.5.
Price was once again found in the second rotated component in
association with the same eight variables as before.

There is great similarity in the factor pattern of the two
stores with respect to welfare-related variables. The emergence of all the locational variables in one component implies
that they are a unique and important evaluative dimension.
That exactly the same pattern emerges for both stores confirms
that locational factors are applicable to both superstores and
hypermarkets.

However, such consistency of factorial patterning is less
evident in the other components and they show considerable
variability between the two stores. For example, the specific
in-store features of bakery and fishmongery at Havant Hypermarket virtually form a separate dimension from all other
constructs. They record high loadings of 0.67 and 0.74 whilst
no other variable has a loading in excess of 0.5 on this component. A similar pattern was not anticipated for ASDA, since
at time of survey, it had no fish sales and this variable
accordingly loads onto component two with the evaluation of
the bakery loading onto component five in association with
'lack of boxes' and 'cleanliness'.

ASDA, WATERLOOVILLE AND HAVANT HYPERMARKET COMPARED
The second major hypothesis was that ASDA should score markedly
better on those constructs relating to welfare. Whilst the principal components analysis has shown that the two stores tended
to display broadly similar factor structures in this respect,

81

Table 5.3
Five varimax-rotated principal components of the perceptual variables – Havant Hypermarket

Stimuli from semantic scale (in order of presentation)	3	2	4	5	1
Very conveniently located	.60				
Often visit other shops on same trip	.75				
Near a family workplace	.71				
In area I often visit	.78				
Good bus links	.59				
A store chain I like		.62			
Prices always low		.64			
Wide range or choice		.67			
Food always fresh		.51			
Good quality items		.72			
Good own-brand range		.69			
Good value overall		.78			
Everything available under one roof		.45			
Goods easy to find		.44			
Staff and services helpful			.41		
Excellent bakery			.67		
Good place to buy fish			.74		
Lack of boxes not a problem				.62	
Easy parking					.62
Good trolley system					.66
Few checkout queues				.65	
Good cheque and credit system					.60
Convenient opening hours					.65
Never blocked by shelf-filling				.54	
Internal layout excellent					.49
Right size of store					.52
Always clean and hygienic					.65
Never too crowded or congested				.63	
Friendly atmosphere					.60
Store temperature just right					.60

(Column header: Loadings on the five components (in order of emergence))

it has not contrasted their performances. To do this it is necessary to look at each of the 30 scales in more detail. The semantic differential required respondents to note how well each store accorded with their evaluation of good location, good bus links and so on. It should be the case that if ASDA had a welfare advantage then it must have scored more highly on the key dimensions. On the other hand, it might be that Havant Hypermarket had advantages in terms of, say, ease of shopping, that made it more appealing to the affluent shopper in this type of area.

Comparison based on modal scores proved difficult since some were bi-modal or tri-modal. Accordingly, it was conceded that a clearer representation could be found by comparing the mean scores. The mean scores were recorded and superimposed on the same scale. This is shown in Table 5.4 and it can be seen that ASDA gains a higher mean score on all five accessibility-related measures and also on the price scale. Nonetheless, Havant Hypermarket was well regarded and had a higher median score than ASDA on 13 evaluations, whilst there are others where they were evenly matched.

The visual interpretation of scores does not, however, reveal whether or not the differences between the stores are random or have statistical significance. Welfare advantages of the district centre location of ASDA have to be demonstrated beyond reasonable doubt. The appropriate technique for testing for significant differences between discrete categories of variables is the χ^2 test. Since all evaluations are based on seven categories there are in all cases six degrees of freedom and the critical value for significance at $p = 0.005$ is 18.55 (Ebdon, 1977). Table 5.5 presents the full list of results for all 30 variables on the semantic scale. These need to be discussed individually since the calculated χ^2 does not always clearly indicate which store gained the better evaluation.

WELFARE ANALYSIS OF ASDA AND HAVANT HYPERMARKET
Since χ^2 cannot be partialled it is conceivable that two stores may differ markedly but in ways such that a welfare difference is not proven. For example, one store might gain a number of extremely high scores but also a number of extremely low scores with the rival store dominating the middle categories. Discovering which had the best overall evaluation might then be difficult. It is essential to show that on the five key locational criteria no such concerns emerge. This is achieved through Table 5.6 which plots the actual scores achieved by each store on the seven-point semantic scale. It can be seen that in every case ASDA gained more scores in the

Table 5.4

Comparison of mean score on evaluations of the thirty perceptual variables – ASDA, Waterlooville and Havant Hypermarket

	Strongly agree	Moderately agree	Slightly agree	Not relevant	Slightly agree	Moderately agree	Strongly agree	
Very conveniently located								Not in a convenient location
Often visit other shops on same trip								Far from other shops I use
Near a family workplace								Not near any family workplace
In area I often visit								Only used if I happen to be near
Good bus links								Poor bus links
A store chain I like								Not a store chain I like
Prices always low								Prices too high
Wide range or choice								Restricted range or choice
Food always fresh								Food not always fresh
Good quality items								Poor quality items
Good own-brand range								Dislike the own-brands
Good value overall								Poor overall value
Everything available under one roof								Cannot buy everything on one trip
Goods easy to find								Goods hard to find
Staff and services helpful								Staff and services unhelpful
Excellent bakery								Poor bakery
Good place to buy fish								Not a place to buy fish
Lack of boxes not a problem								Lack of boxes a major problem
Easy parking								Parking not easy
Good trolley system								Bad trolley system
Few checkout queues								Always checkout queues
Good cheque and credit system								Poor cheque and credit system
Convenient opening hours								Inconvenient opening hours
Never blocked by shelf-filling								Re-stocking often in progress
Internal layout excellent								Poor internal layout
Right size of store								Store wrong size for me
Always clean and hygienic								Not clean or hygienic
Never too crowded or congested								Always crowded and congested
Friendly atmosphere								Unfriendly atmosphere
Store temperature just right								Store temperature wrong

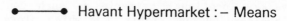

●━━━━━━● Havant Hypermarket : – Means

●·········● ASDA Waterlooville : – Means

Table 5.5
χ^2 Analysis of the thirty semantic variables comparing
ASDA, Waterlooville, and Havant Hypermarket

Variable number	Variable	Calculated χ^2	Level of Significance
1	"Very conveniently located"	60.12	$p < 0.005$
2	"Visit near other shops on same trip"	246.89	$p < 0.005$
3	"Near family workplace"	6.79	$p > 0.005$
4	"In area I often visit"	149.55	$p < 0.005$
5	"Good bus links"	77.77	$p < 0.005$
6	"Store chain I like"	2.98	$p > 0.005$
7	"Prices always low"	25.69	$p < 0.005$
8	"Wide range of choice"	19.69	$p < 0.005$
9	"Goods always fresh"	23.67	$p < 0.005$
10	"Good quality items"	12.01	$p > 0.005$
11	"Good own-brand range"	38.83	$p < 0.005$
12	"Good value overall"	10.41	$p > 0.005$
13	"All under one roof"	69.52	$p < 0.005$
14	"Goods easy to find"	5.58	$p > 0.005$
15	"Staff and service helpful"	10.58	$p > 0.005$
16	Evaluation of 'bakery' not possible		
17	"Good place to buy fish"	205.19	$p < 0.005$
18	"Lack of boxes not a problem"	5.38	$p > 0.005$

Table 5.5 (Continued)

Variable number	Variable	Calculated χ^2	Level of Significance
19	Evaluation of 'parking' not possible		
20	"Good trolley system"	34.68	$p < 0.005$
21	"Few checkout queues"	17.66	$p > 0.005$
22	Evaluation of 'good cheque and credit system' not possible		
23	Evaluation of 'convenient opening hours' not possible		
24	"Not blocked by shelf filling"	10.08	$p > 0.005$
25	"Internal layout excellent"	13.49	$p > 0.005$
26	"Right size of store"	21.26	$p < 0.005$
27	Evaluation of 'always clean and hygienic' not possible		
28	"Never too crowded or congested"	11.62	$p > 0.005$
29	"Friendly atmosphere"	12.45	$p > 0.005$
30	"Store temperature just right"	13.67	$p > 0.005$

df = 6, critical value at $p < 0.005$ is 18.55

Table 5.6
Comparison of number of responses in each category for the 7-point evaluation of locational factors, ASDA, Waterlooville and Havant Hypermarket

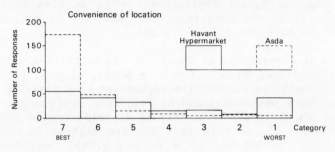

Convenience of location

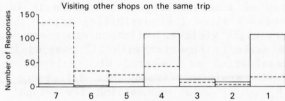

Visiting other shops on the same trip

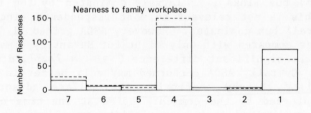

Nearness to family workplace

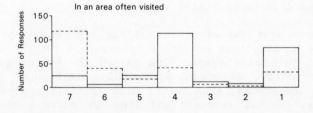

In an area often visited

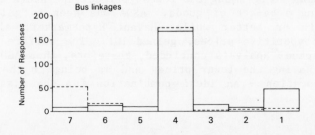

Bus linkages

'best' category (7) and fewer in the 'worst' category (1). In terms of nearness to family workplace, however, the middle category dominates both distributions and suggests that this is not a relevant issue for shoppers in this area. Since neither ASDA nor Havant Hypermarket is in an area with major workplaces, it is not surprising that the χ^2 is not significant (χ^2 = 6.79. df = 6, p > 0.005).

In terms of convenience of location, the better evaluations of ASDA were confirmed by χ^2 (χ^2 = 60.12, df = 6, p < 0.005) and seem strongly to support the advantages of a district centre location. This was compounded by 'visiting other shops on the same trip' which related directly to district centre shopping. The calculated χ^2 in this case was the highest in the whole analysis (χ^2 = 246.89, df = 6, p < 0.005) confirming the welfare dimension of accessibility. If a store is in an area which is frequently visited the possibility arises that disadvantaged shoppers might visit it whilst on other errands. Here again, ASDA was markedly superior with 117 respondents giving ASDA a 'best' evaluation as compared with only 24 at Havant Hypermarket. Tests again confirmed this difference (χ^2 = 149.55, df = 6, p < 0.005) emphasising the visual results obtained in Tables 5.2 and 5.4. The final accessibility measure, 'good bus links', is largely dominated by the impression that this is not relevant to most respondents since the middle 'neutral' box dominates. However, ASDA gained 51 'best' evaluations as compared with only eight for Havant Hypermarket, a statistically significant difference (χ^2 = 77.77, df = 6, p < 0.005). Overall, ASDA performed markedly better in terms of accessibility thereby confirming its welfare advantages. This was reinforced by the comments noted at the time of the survey which emphasised that accessibility is a key issue as many perceived ASDA to be better placed.

Attention was next turned to the factor 'prices always low' since this is an important welfare consideration for the disadvantaged. In this case again, ASDA gained the better evaluation (χ^2 = 25.69, df = 6, p < 0.005). ASDA has always promoted its low prices (ASDA PRICE) with specific emphasis on branded goods. Market research and consumer surveys consistently show ASDA to be among the lowest-priced superstore chains for purchasing a basket of goods. ASDA was seen to gain 141 scores of six or better whilst Havant Hypermarket, also a store with competitive prices, gained 101. The welfare basis of the perceptual analysis concluded, therefore, that ASDA was regarded as having the lower prices and as being in the more accessible location - an ideal combination for the disadvantaged shopper.

OTHER DIMENSIONS OF STORE COMPARISON

The results so far all demonstrated the welfare advantages of
the district centre location of ASDA. This confirms the impression gained in Chapter four, where store patrons were interviewed, that ASDA is simply more accessible and also facili-
tates other types of shopping trip. It must however, be remem-
bered that the semantic scales contain many other variables
that were seen as important in the overall shopping experience.
It should be recalled that the concept of relative disadvantage applies most often not when a local facility is lost but
when a new and favoured facility is sited so remotely that one
cannot benefit from it. Within the patterns of variation
among the remaining variables Havant Hypermarket might display
many features to which the less mobile consumer would like to
gain access. This would be demonstrated in any instance where
Havant Hypermarket gained markedly better evaluations than
ASDA.

This wider evaluation began with consideration of the concept
'a store chain I like'. Here, both stores performed very well
indeed though there are some problems with this concept. This
was only the second ASDA store in the region though the chain
is much better known in the north of England. Though a divi-
sion of Portsea Island Mutual Co-operative (PIMCO), Havant
Hypermarket was regarded by that chain as a separately-func-
tioning entity. The Co-operative link was not emphasised in
advertising; the Co-op logo was not prominently displayed and
the store had a unique image. It seemed most probable that
respondents were using this measure to express their personal
approval of the two stores. If that was the case, then the
stores were well liked for a majority of responses in each
case fell in the highest categories and, because of this, the
result was not significant (χ^2 = 2.98, df = 6, p< 0.005).
Reservations could be expressed with regard to the results on
the concept 'wide range or choice'. Havant Hypermarket is the
larger store and gained 133 'best' evaluations to ASDA's 94.
However, in the next most favoured category, it was ASDA that
dominated and when the two categories were combined the calculated test statistic fell below the critical level of significance. Because χ^2 was initially significant (χ^2 =
19.69, df = 6, p < 0.005), it had to be presumed that Havant
Hypermarket was marginally the preferred store.

A similar problem recurred with 'food always fresh' since in
this case Havant Hypermarket out-performed ASDA in the two top
categories but ASDA dominated the next. This again cast doubt
on the significant association (χ^2 = 23.67, df = 6, p
<0.005) and it should be noted that 85 percent of respondents
viewed food freshness favourably at Havant Hypermarket, and 84

percent at ASDA. No difference could be discerned for 'good quality items' (χ^2 = 12.01, df = 6, p > 0.005) but a significant difference emerged with respect to own brands (χ^2 = 38.83, df = 6, p < 0.005). Havant Hypermarket, retailing Co-op branded goods as own-brand, gained the favourable evaluation and this may reflect ASDA's traditional orientation toward branded goods. Of late, ASDA has begun to recognise the own-brand trend emphasised by J. Sainsbury PLC and has expanded its own-brand range.

In respect of 'everything available under one roof' Havant Hypermarket was favoured with 178 'best' evaluations to ASDA's 90 (χ^2 = 69.52, df = 6, p < 0.005). However, neither 'goods easy to find' nor 'staff and services helpful' produced significant results. Evaluations of the respective bakeries were hampered by a separate problem. So few individuals gave a low evaluation at either store that the distribution of responses infringed the requirements of χ^2. At this point, then, it was useful to recall that Table 6.6 compared mean evaluations of the two stores and showed that Havant Hypermarket was slightly ahead in this respect. The point was confirmed by the finding that 87.5 percent of respondents viewed its bakery favourably as compared with 83.5 percent at ASDA. The consistent picture to emerge was of a comparison of two very favourably regarded stores where one would occasionally gain an even better evaluation than the other.

Reservations about which store was preferred were dispelled when the question of fish sales arose. At time of interview, ASDA had no fresh fish sales and it would, therefore, have been remarkable had Havant Hypermarket not been preferred. As it was, the test statistic was second only to 'often visit other shops on the same trip', being highly significant (χ^2 = 205.19, df = 6, p < 0.005). However, from this point onward, evaluations were difficult to test statistically. Neither store provided boxes for carrying away goods and no significant difference emerged though 26 percent of ASDA shoppers felt inconvenienced by this as opposed to 19 percent at Havant Hypermarket. Ease of parking could not be tested since only one person gave a negative evaluation of parking at Havant Hypermarket and only 25 at ASDA. Though shopping trolleys were complained about under 'likes and dislikes' (Chapter 5), it is clear that ASDA trolleys were so much more disliked that a significant difference emerged (χ^2 = 34.86, df = 6, p <0.005). As noted, this is probably because the shopper does not retain the same trolley throughout the trip at ASDA. This may inconvenience those with small children who may be forced to switch, at the checkout, to a trolley without a babyseat.

The topics in this part of the analysis have addressed the issues surrounding the ease or comfort of the shopping trip and there may be a welfare implication in this. Queueing at checkouts may be a major irritant to shoppers and Table 5.5 showed Havant Hypermarket to be slightly more favoured in this respect. Certainly, it gains more evaluations than ASDA in the 'best' category and fewer in the 'worst', but this is not statistically significant. Neither 'cheque and credit system' nor 'opening hours' gained sufficient negative responses at either store to permit χ^2 analysis and Table 5.4 shows how close the two store types were on these measures. Nor did 'shelf-filling' produce a significant association though Table 5.4 shows that Havant Hypermarket scored more highly in terms of mean evaluation.

The viewpoint that both stores were well-favoured with regard to non-welfare issues is consistently emphasised by Table 5.4. Only rarely did either store gain a mean evaluation on the negative side of the scale. In terms of 'internal layout' the two stores were well matched, with 79 percent viewing this aspect favourably at ASDA and 76.5 percent at Havant Hypermarket. The two stores follow very closely the standard practise of requiring shoppers to pass through the non-food sections, where they might impulse purchase, before reaching the food section. Whilst no difference emerged in respect of internal layout, there was a perceived difference regarding the respective sizes of the two stores (χ^2 = 21.26, df = 6, p <0.005). It would appear that the ASDA size of store is preferred, since 79.5 percent of respondents gave a favourable response as opposed to 67.5 percent for Havant Hypermarket. It is certainly the case that, for some individuals, the hypermarket format may simply be too big for comfortable shopping. With regard to cleanliness and hygiene, the results were overwhelmingly favourable, with 91 percent viewing ASDA positively and 89 percent viewing Havant Hypermarket positively. This pattern was repeated in respect of store congestion, atmosphere and temperature and re-emphasised the close competition between these two stores.

SUMMARY OF RESEARCH FINDINGS
This chapter set out to test two key hypotheses: whether or not welfare issues really were important to shoppers and the extent to which the two stores differed in such respects. The balance of evidence from three separate types of data analysis suggests that welfare matters are important. Evidence would imply that ASDA could improve its trolley system and that such a store genuinely does need ample parking.

CONCLUSIONS

Aside from the empirical support for the research hypothesis, the work reported in this chapter has shown clearly that a 'subjective social indicators' approach is a useful procedure. It was noted that by no means all of the 260 individuals who responded to the questionnaire had chosen to shop at ASDA or Havant Hypermarket. They had, however, a capacity to evaluate the two stores using perceptual techniques and those techniques produced welfare-relevant results. The respondents were merely required to evaluate one hypermarket and one superstore using objectively derived measures. These two formats are the ones that will dominate large-scale grocery retailing for the foreseeable future. Figure 5.1 shows the distribution of those respondents from the 260 who had made ASDA or Havant Hypermarket their 'main store'. Clearly, the impact is considerable and most individuals in the zone of equidistance must have given serious consideration to making use of these stores.

As yet in this study little emphasis has been placed upon disadvantaged individuals for whom the welfare issues thus far identified will be of crucial concern. Disadvantaged individuals will have responded to the surveys undertaken in this Chapter and in Chapter four, but no attempt has as yet been made to separate them from the general mass of consumers in order to discern their special characteristics separately, if such exist. This is a key objective of the next chapter since it has now been clearly demonstrated that welfare-relevant issues are important to consumers in the area and that ASDA gained the better evaluations. These results serve to confirm the pattern of findings established in Chapter four. Throughout the empirical research to this point there has been ample evidence that ASDA's location in a district centre confers all-important virtues of accessibility. Despite the costs and penalties of such a location, ASDA has been able to provide goods to the shoppers at prices that were viewed as more competitive than those at Havant Hypermarket.

At the same time, it was recognised that not all constructs used by individuals when choosing between stores are, in fact, welfare or accessibility-related in the strictest sense of the term. All 30 constructs on the semantic differential scales were objectively derived and the bulk of them did not directly relate to welfare considerations. However, the research was cast in such a way that all the variables had some relevance to disadvantage. If a favourable feature of shopping was provided by one store but not by another, then this could be seen as an element of relative disadvantage. Consequently, wherever Havant Hypermarket was more favourably viewed than ASDA, an aspect of relative disadvantage was found and was, on occasion, confirmed statistically.

Shoppers using:-

● ASDA
○ Havant Hypermarket

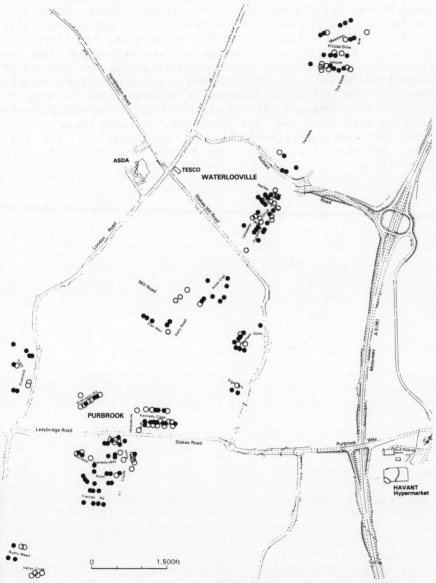

Figure 5.1 Home locations of those respondents participating
in perceptual evaluation and claiming to use either ASDA,
Waterlooville, or Havant Hypermarket.

Facets worthy of note in this respect included the much better evaluation of Havant Hypermarket because of its fresh fish sales. This is the type of facility that perhaps should be insisted upon by planners when such stores are developed. A similar result was found in respect of 'range or choice' where Havant Hypermarket was again slightly ahead. This need not imply a requirement for stores of full hypermarket size but it does lend weight to the ASDA requirement for floorspace in excess of 4,000 m^2. 'Range or choice' might just as clearly be related to a perceived under-supply of 'own-brand' goods at ASDA and upon this the chain are known to be responding. In the following chapter an attempt will be made to show how disadvantaged individuals react to the shopping opportunities with which they are presented. Already there is evidence that welfare-related factors are important and that ASDA, Waterlooville gains the better evaluations in such respects.

6 Social and welfare aspects of shopping in the study area

INTRODUCTION

The preceding two chapters have laid the basis for a welfare analysis of hypermarkets and superstores. Chapter four showed that these store types differed in terms of the person attracted and in terms of shopping-trip characteristics. Chapter five showed that a 'subjective social indicators' approach using perceptual techniques could illustrate measurable welfare differences between such stores. It was necessary, however, to pinpoint the disadvantaged shopper and discover how such a person would behave when presented with a nearby superstore and hypermarket. This task was not an easy one given the nature of the detailed study area (see Figure 1.2). It has already been emphasised that this is a suburban area in southern England where extremely high levels of disadvantage are not to be expected. It was even feared that no enumeration districts might be found where shoppers were highly constrained in their shopping behaviour. Furthermore, there is the simple fact that shopping can also be a 'social' activity and this might imply that some people direct their shopping behaviour to that end.

It was expected that disadvantage would most probably be expressed in terms of relative disadvantage. This would tend to emphasise factors such as driving-licence possession and car availability, as well as background factors such as old age or immobility. Likewise, full attention would have to be paid to 'social' factors of shopping. The major initial problem was, however, the definition of a suitable study area and this is now outlined.

STUDY AREA

Theoretically it would have been possible to undertake the analysis of 'social' and 'welfare' criteria anywhere in the general study area. In order to retain a comparison between the superstore and hypermarket modes of shopping, however, it was decided that an approach attempting a full welfare-type analysis had to remain within the catchment areas of the two stores. One implication of this decision might be that no very disadvantaged groups would be identified. At the same time it was regarded as important to adopt an approach that was as universal as possible, rather than one which was totally dependent upon disadvantaged groups being present. On the other hand, if evidence of some form of disadvantage could be found even here, then the importance of the concept is reinforced. In order to identify the most fruitful areas for analysis, reference was made to the 1981 Census returns for the area. It was found that for the 1981 Census 47 enumeration districts (EDs) fell within 3 km of the two stores. The characteristics of households within those areas that were deemed to be of interest for welfare purposes were:
1) Households with residents aged under 15; 2) Households with unemployed persons; 3) Households in local authority housing; 4) Households in owner-occupation; 5) Households with no car; 6) Households with two or more cars; 7) Households with pensioners; 8) Households with 3 or more children; 9) Households with children and no car. Such variables correlate with household income but also have specific applicability to shopping.

It was felt that such measures would pinpoint low income and, equally, high income areas within the study area. The 47 EDs included areas of total owner-occupation and areas of total local authority ownership. Very few households, it may be noted, had dependent children but no car available. The range of car availability ran from sixty percent of households with no car to just four percent. Only in four enumeration districts did more than half of the households have no car.

It was decided that, since welfare had so far been cast in accessibility terms, any areas chosen had to remain roughly equidistant between the two stores. This greatly restricted the range of suitable EDs and emphasised again the areas covered in the preceding chapter. It was decided that areas containing individuals who were as disadvantaged as possible in respect of

the selected census variables should be chosen. To highlight
the contrast, areas containing individuals who were advantaged
in terms of those same variables were also chosen.

For purposes of defining areas where lower income and higher
income individuals were most likely to be found, EDs AP10,
AP11, AP12, AM10 and AM11 were chosen and these are indicated
in Figure 6.1. It can be seen that they are as nearly equidistant from the two stores as is possible. AP10, AP11 and
AP12 had an almost total absence of local authority housing,
were in the top six for car ownership, were the top three for
ownership of more than one car, and also registered very
low levels of unemployment. AM10 was the ED with the lowest
car ownership figures in the whole sample area, AM11 had the
greatest incidence of large families, whilst both areas were
overwhelmingly in local authority tenure in 1981. AM10 also
scored highly on pensioner households, but this remained the
most weakly-represented welfare variable. ED AK08, with the
highest count of pensioner households, was at the fringe of
the study area and markedly more accessible to the ASDA store,
so it was felt that the five EDs chosen gave the best representation of the range of welfare variables available.

It was decided to sample all the households falling within
the chosen EDs that were also approximately equidistant between
the two stores. Whilst it is obviously the case that not all
persons in a low income area are low income individuals, the
chances of finding such persons are greatly increased. The EDs
contained a total of 959 households but the precise pattern of
streets meant that some households were markedly nearer to ASDA.
This was especially the case with the 600 higher income households which were located on the eastern fringe of Waterlooville.
Quite simply, no houses existed further east in the direction
of Havant Hypermarket. Some 189 of the 201 households in AP11
were so much closer to ASDA than to Havant Hypermarket that they
could not possibly be regarded as 'equidistant' on any criterion. It was finally decided that 260 households, or 27 percent
of the total in the EDs, maximised the locational requirements.
Half were in the higher income area and half in the lower income
area and a full census of all these households was attempted.
After multiple repeat visits and the option of mailing back the
questionnaire, 113 higher income households (87 percent of those
approached) and 88 lower income households (67 percent of those
approached) made a response. This constituted 21 percent of all
households in the five sample EDs. It was still felt that some
of the higher income residents were slightly closer to ASDA than
to Havant Hypermarket. Fortunately, the more important lower
income EDs which were central to the welfare analysis were very
close to being equidistant from the two two stores.

97

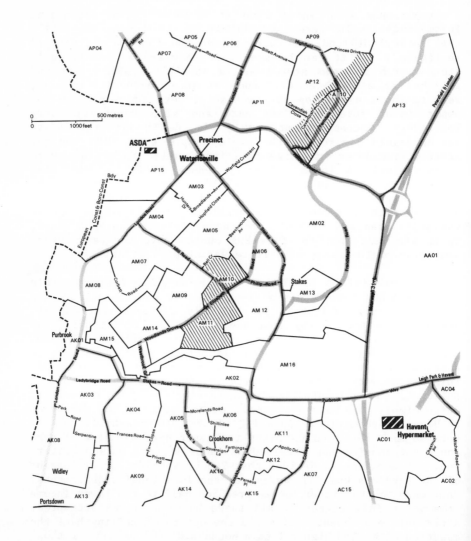

\\\\\\\ E.D.ˢ Selected for study

Figure 6.1 Relationship of enumeration districts selected for th
welfare analysis, to ASDA, Waterlooville, and Havant Hypermarket

98

THE QUESTIONNAIRE

In order to test both social and welfare aspects of the shopping experience, a questionnaire was devised which covered all possible dimensions of these aspects yet remained sufficiently simple for the respondents to answer. The questionnaire sought to gain basic information such as which store was, in fact, the main grocery store for respondents since it was already proven that stores other than ASDA, Waterlooville and Havant Hypermarket were used by shoppers in the area. The prime example was the Tesco supermarket in Waterlooville and reference has already been made to the likelihood that the lower income shopper has come to rely on the high street supermarket for lower prices. Since the Tesco store had been trading for many years it was bound to have considerable customer loyalty even though the 'impact study' demonstrated that ASDA diverted much custom from this store. Nor should it be forgotten that the perceptual evaluations showed that many found Havant Hypermarket to be 'too big' and there were probably also those who found ASDA to be too big a store. That Tesco, Waterlooville continued to trade successfully when the company had been aggressively closing similar outlets of just that size was testimony to the fact that it still had a market locally. Furthermore, Tesco was the only outlet in Waterlooville for those wishing to shop at supermarkets, since the former Co-op and Shoppers Paradise stores had closed.

Accordingly, the simple question as to which store was used - supplemented by a question on other stores used - was sandwiched between the other more substantive parts of the questionnaire. The questionnaire began by addressing the social aspects of shopping and relied heavily on variables used previously by Bruce (1974), Bowlby (1979) and Guy (1984b). The most common method for the presentation of such variables has been through a 5, 7, or 9 point rating scale. The former was chosen in this case since this had been used successfully by previous researchers on this topic and pilot studies confirmed the acceptability of a 5-point scale. It was felt that the range of questions was sufficiently wide to give an adequate representation of the many possible ways in which shopping may be viewed as not simply an economic exercise.

The latter part of the questionnaire was devoted to the gathering of such information on the background of the shoppers as would permit a welfare-based appraisal, possibly a Lorenz approach, to be undertaken. There were questions on car ownership, driving licence holding and mode of travel to the chosen store. The demands of those who had to fit shopping in around work, or allow for the demands of small children and the elderly, were also catered for and social status was to be estimated from occupation. It was felt that little more could possibly be asked without making the questionnaire unwieldy or straining the good will of respondents. These questions were to form the basis of a welfare analysis and will be referred to subsequently as the welfare variables.

SOCIAL ASPECTS OF SHOPPING

For two main reasons, 'social' aspects of shopping deserved consideration before other parts of the extensive questionnaire survey. The first of these was that they might undermine the whole basis of the remainder of the analysis. On census night, 1981, every ED surveyed had at least 40 percent of households with one car or more. This gave rise to the real possibility that most shoppers could exercise a great amount of flexibility as to where they shopped. With weak constraints to shopping, social aspects might come to the fore and it was not known what differences, if any, would emerge between the lower income and higher income individuals. A final reason for treating the 'social' aspects separately was that they were elicited in a different manner from those in the rest of the questionnaire. Other aspects surveyed were essentially geared to gathering factual information. The 'social' aspects were cast as a rating scale akin to the semantic differential used in the previous chapter. This required that they be analysed by techniques different from those appropriate to later parts of the questionnaire.

In order to gain a 'feel' for the data the responses to the 22 scales were initially cast as histograms (Figure 6.2). The common tendency in social surveys, to avoid the extreme categories, can be observed in the histograms. That said, there are two instances where the extreme categories are well used. These demonstrated that the vast majority did not agree that 'the convenience of local shops is worth the extra it can cost' nor that 'price is not important' to them. When attention was turned to the general balance of responses between the favourable and the unfavourable then it could be seen that some questions roughly divided the sample. An instance of this was the question of finding shopping 'a nuisance' and wanting to get it done quickly. In other cases, the balance was definitely negative, a prime example of this being 'I prefer to shop at the 'small man' type of shop' since it was clear that this sample of respondents most certainly did not. A more positive set of responses was generated by such questions as 'I always try to buy good quality food, even if prices are higher' and most claimed to do this though there was almost certainly a 'halo' effect here. This response may be related to the general agreement that price is important to people and that 'chain stores and supermarkets make for better grocery shopping all round'.

100

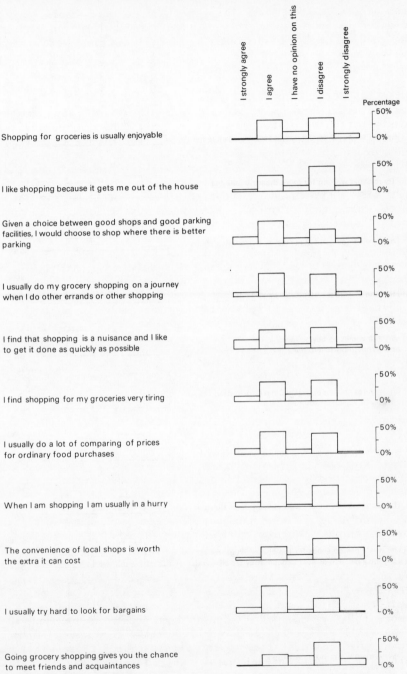

Figure 6.2 Histograms of percentage responses to questions on 'social' aspects of shopping

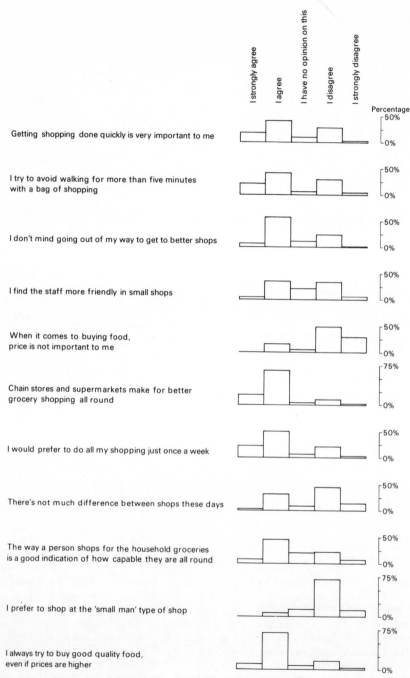

Getting shopping done quickly is very important to me

I try to avoid walking for more than five minutes with a bag of shopping

I don't mind going out of my way to get to better shops

I find the staff more friendly in small shops

When it comes to buying food, price is not important to me

Chain stores and supermarkets make for better grocery shopping all round

I would prefer to do all my shopping just once a week

There's not much difference between shops these days

The way a person shops for the household groceries is a good indication of how capable they are all round

I prefer to shop at the 'small man' type of shop

I always try to buy good quality food, even if prices are higher

I strongly agree

I agree

I have no opinion on this

I disagree

I strongly disagree

Figure 6.2 (continued)

This set of questions was not without its problems and some doubt must be cast over the validity of the question 'I like shopping because it gets me out of the house'. It might have been preferable in the present context to have stressed grocery shopping rather than shopping in general. The appropriate approach for the analysis of these questions was principal components analysis of the scales. The reasons for this were broadly the same as those put forward for the perceptual analysis in the previous chapter. The large amount of data just on social factors, though fewer than in the perceptual analysis, gave nearly 4,500 separate pieces of information. It was intuitively felt that the 22 scales would probably form a structure of sub-scales, as before, if a grouping procedure were applied. Identification of sub-scales, rather than general dimensions of the data set, is a characteristic of principal components analysis with varimax rotation. It was therefore decided that this technique should be used in a similar manner to that outlined in Chapter five.

SUB-ELEMENTS OF 'SOCIAL' FACTORS IN SHOPPING
The clearest possible presentation of the major components to emerge from the varimax rotation, through a ranked listing of the factors, is shown in Table 6.1. This demonstrates the order in which the factors emerged, the important loadings and the intuitive labels that were applied to them. Interpretation of the factors, though subjective, was a vital exercise. It might be that some key 'social' aspects of shopping would cut across lines of 'advantage' and 'disadvantage' in a study region such as this. The crucial point was whether or not the dimensions that emerged would divide on welfare lines or transcend them. Labels were therefore attached to the factors in order to identify them and particular attention was paid to factors that were polarised in that they had both high positive and high negative loadings. This would identify factors where variables gained contrasting responses and represented opposite poles of a shopping scale.

Each factor was considered in turn. The first major component to emerge was labelled 'enjoyment' where respondents who gained enjoyment from shopping were contrasted with those who found it a nuisance or were in a hurry. The second component was labelled 'price' as all the variables relating to price loaded heavily on it. Note, too, that a positive loading was found with the assessment of those who identified with being 'capable all round' so there was a clear element of thriftiness here. The third component related to the 'small' and 'local' shopping factors which are a distinct element in the shopping system. The fourth component seemed to emphasise parking, use of the car as a mobile shopping basket, and those stores that

Table 6.1 Varimax-rotated factor matrix on attitudes towards shopping

Loadings on components in order of emergence

Stimulus	Factor 1 Enjoyment	Factor 2 Price	Factor 3 Small and Local	Factor 4 Parking	Factor 5 Sociability	Factor 6 Quality
Shopping for groceries is usually enjoyable	0.79321					
I like shopping because it gets me out of the house	0.71600					
I find that shopping is a nuisance and I like to get it done as quickly as possible	-0.87954					
Getting shopping done quickly is very important to me	-0.75366					
When I am shopping I am usually in a hurry	-0.66492					
I find shopping for my groceries very tiring	-0.62805					
I would prefer to do all my shopping just once a week	-0.41739					
When it comes to buying food, price not important to me		-0.58384				
I usually do a lot of comparing of prices for ordinary food prices		0.80809				
I usually try hard to look for bargains		0.79733				
The way a person shops for the household groceries is a good indication of how capable they are all round		0.52761				
I prefer to shop at the 'small-man' type of shop			0.70183			
The convenience of local shops is worth the extra it can cost			0.69076			
I find the staff more friendly in small shops			0.61031			
Given a choice between good shops and good parking facilities, I would choose to shop where there is better parking				0.71547		
I try to avoid walking for more than five minues with a bag of shopping				0.58862		
Chain stores and supermarkets make for better grocery shopping all round				0.54057		
I usually do my grocery shopping on a journey when I do other errands or other shopping					0.61304	
There's not much difference between shops these days					0.58658	
Going grocery shopping gives you the chance to meet friends and acquaintances					0.43107	
I always try to buy good quality food, even if prices are higher						0.78396
I don't mind going out of my way to get to better shops						0.57990

emphasised 'parking' as an element in their attraction. Component five identified those individuals who did not value shopping as an activity but saw it as a means to an end or an adjunct to other activities. Finally, component six identified the quality of shopping available. If proof be needed that shopping is something more than a simple welfare-related function of everyday life then these results have surely provided that evidence. Enjoyment of shopping was counterpointed with tiring or hurried shopping and regarding price as unimportant contrasted well with bargain hunting and price-comparison. Those factors that have both high positive and high negative loadings particularly served to suggest that real dimensions of contrasted behaviour have been elicited by the variables chosen. What is crucial for present purposes is that factors of price and parking emerged as clearly identifiable dimensions.

THE WELFARE VARIABLES
With clear evidence of the validity of 'social' variables, some of which might apply equally to lower income and higher income shoppers, attention was next turned to the remaining 21 variables. These were not cast as a rating scale but provided evidence on actual shopping habits. Since some of these welfare-related variables might also span the two groups of shopper types, it was decided again to consider the variables at an aggregate level before proceeding to disaggregate and statistically analyse them. This approach offered the further advantage of giving a picture of the characteristics of the study area as a whole. It was already anticipated that little 'absolute' disadvantage would be found. If demonstrable differences in terms of relative disadvantage could be found in an area such as this then the concept itself would be reinforced.

A crucial question lay with the determination of which grocery stores would be preferred by the respondents in this zone of equidistance. Evidence on main grocery store used, as shown in Table 6.2, and stores sometimes used, as shown in Table 6.3, pointed to the dominance of ASDA. With Tesco, Waterlooville, being the second most popular main store, the advantages of the district centre location were further emphasised. Waitrose in Cowplain centre was also frequently mentioned though this store was markedly nearer to the higher income area. The wide range of stores mentioned could be seen as a token of the competitiveness of the retail grocery trade in an area such as this. It was also seen as a measure of the loyalty of individuals to their 'preferred' stores despite the addition of two major outlets. Mode of transport to the store was seen as a crucial welfare dimension, (Table 6.4) and this showed the car to be overwhelmingly dominant. It was revealed that only 15 households in the total sample had no car (Table 6.5).

Table 6.2
Frequency distribution of respondents by main grocery store used

Main grocery store used	Number of respondents	Percentage of respondents
ASDA	97	48.5
Havant Hypermarket	28	14.0
Other multiple	1	0.5
Tesco	38	19.0
Waitrose	27	13.5
Sainsbury	3	1.5
Independent	4	2.0
Cooperative	1	0.5
No response	2	1.0
TOTALS =	201	100.5

Table 6.3
Frequency distribution of respondents by other store sometimes used

Other grocery store sometimes used	Number of respondents	Percentage of respondents
ASDA	38	19.0
Havant Hypermarket	35	17.5
Other multiple	2	1.0
Tesco	57	28.5
Waitrose	27	13.5
Sainsbury	9	4.5
Independent	12	6.0
Cooperative	5	2.5
No response	16	8.0
TOTALS =	201	100.5

Table 6.4
Frequency distribution of respondents by mode of
transport to main grocery store

Mode	Number of respondents	Percentage of respondents
Foot	34	17.0
Cycle	2	1.0
Motorcycle	1	0.5
Bus	6	3.0
Car	158	78.5
TOTALS =	201	100.0

Table 6.5
Frequency distribution of respondents by number of cars in the household

Number of cars	Number of respondents	Percentage of respondents
None	15	7.5
One	112	55.5
Two	62	31.0
Three or more	12	6.0
TOTALS =	201	100.0

This reinforced the importance both of 'social' factors and of the 'perceptual' evaluations analysed in Chapter five. The likelihood of 'absolute' disadvantage being found in the study area was diminished by the high levels of car ownership.

What the first batch of variables revealed was that ASDA, in a district centre, had to be able to attract car owners and car users in an area where the population was highly mobile. On the other hand it was revealed that only seven shoppers felt disadvantaged by not being being able to reach Havant Hypermarket (Table 6.6). Far more shoppers felt disadvantaged by virtue of not having a nearby Sainsbury outlet. Subsequent tables offer some detail on accessibility factors, with Table 6.7 revealing that, though 92.5 percent of households sampled had a car, only 63 percent had a car available for shopping at all times. Such facts are important features of 'relative' disadvantage, confirming the validity of not relying upon car ownership figures alone. A similar pattern emerged with respect to possession of a driving licence. It emerged that only 67.5 percent of those responsible for the family grocery shopping also had a licence (Table 6.8). When a breakdown was made of the times of day when shopping was undertaken it was seen that the morning dominated (Table 6.9) and this also may be related to car availability.

Further detail on the study area comes from the revelation that the two-adult household was the dominant pattern (Table 6.10). Slightly more than half of the total households sampled had children present (Table 6.11) but few of these children were under the age of five (Table 6.12). This would seem to reduce further the likelihood of finding individuals who were severely disadvantaged through having to shop whilst coping with small children. Table 6.13 elaborates upon this by revealing that only 25 households had to take children out shopping, or chose so to do. The suspicion that few pensioners would be found is confirmed by Table 6.14 which shows that only 18 percent of households had pensioners present. Further evidence comes from Table 6.15 where only 15.5 percent of those responsible for shopping were found to be over 60. Otherwise, there was a good spread of ages among the shoppers surveyed, though the age band 30-50 supplied over half of the respondents. The picture that emerged was one of a mobile, young to middle-aged population with grown children. Second incomes were prevalent, as Table 6.16 on 'fitting in shopping around work' records. This impression is reinforced by Tables 6.17 and 6.18 which offer data on part-time and shift working. Second incomes distort the relationship between the household income and the status of the head of the household. This was noteworthy since occupation was to be used as a surrogate for social status and, by implication, wealth.

Table 6.6
Frequency distribution of respondents by grocery store stated as too difficult to reach

Store name	Number of respondents	Percentage of respondents
Havant Hypermarket	7	11.0
Other multiple	11	17.0
Waitrose	2	3.0
Sainsbury	43	67.0
Cooperative	1	1.5
TOTALS =	64	99.5

Table 6.7
Frequency distribution of respondents by car
availability for shopping

Car availability	Number of respondents	Percentage of respondents
All the time	127	63.0
Evenings only	9	5.0
Evenings and weekends only	28	14.0
Weekends only	7	3.5
Other/no response	30	15.0
TOTALS =	201	100.5

Table 6.8
Frequency distribution of respondents by possession of a full driving licence

Possession of full licence	Number of respondents	Percentage of respondents
Yes	136	67.5
No	62	30.5
No response	3	1.5
TOTALS =	201	99.5

Table 6.9
Frequency distribution of respondents by
time of day chosen for shopping

Time of day for shopping	Number of respondents	Percentage of respondents
Before midday	104	51.5
Midday to 5pm	58	29.0
After 5pm	39	19.5
TOTALS =	201	100.0

Table 6.10
Frequency distribution of respondents by number
of adults in the household

Number of adults	Number of respondents	Percentage of respondents
One	16	8.0
Two	140	70.0
Three	34	17.0
Four or more	11	5.5
TOTALS =	201	100.5

Table 6.11
Frequency distribution of respondents by number of children present in the household

Number of children stated as present	Number of respondents	Percentage of respondents
None	81	40.5
One	36	18.0
Two	59	29.5
Three	18	9.0
Four or more	4	2.0
No response	3	1.5
TOTALS =	201	100.5

Table 6.12
Frequency distribution of respondents by numbers of children under five years of age stated as being present in the household

Number of children stated as present	Number of respondents	Percentage of respondents
None	156	77.5
One	21	10.5
Two	9	4.5
Three	1	0.5
No response	14	7.0
TOTALS =	201	100.0

Table 6.13
Frequency distribution of respondents with
children, in respect of children being present
on the shopping trip

Children present on shopping trip	Number of respondents	Percentage of respondents
Yes	25	78.0
No	7	22.0
TOTALS =	32	100.0

Table 6.14
Frequency distribution of respondents by numbers of pensioners in the household

Number of pensioners	Number of respondents	Percentage of respondents
None	146	72.5
One	18	9.0
Two	17	8.5
Three	2	1.0
No response	18	9.0
TOTALS =	201	100.0

Table 6.15
Frequency distribution of respondents by age group

Age group	Number of respondents	Percentage of respondents
Under 30	26	13.0
30-39	54	27.0
40-49	51	25.5
50-59	39	19.5
Over 60	31	15.5
TOTALS =	201	100.5

Table 6.16
Frequency distribution of respondents in
respect of fitting in shopping around work

Shopping fitted around work	Number of respondents	Percentage of respondents
Yes	96	48.0
No	103	51.0
No response	2	1.0
TOTALS =	201	100.0

Table 6.17
Frequency distribution of respondents who work in respect of type of work done

Type of work	Number of respondents	Percentage of respondents
Full-time	48	49.5
Part-time	49	50.5
TOTALS =	97	100.0

Table 6.18
Frequency distribution of respondents who
work in respect of shift working

Shift work done	Number of respondents	Percentage of respondents
Yes	14	14.5
No	83	85.5
TOTALS =	97	100.0

The results of translating occupational information into broad social class groups is shown in Table 6.19. When occupation of head of household was sought only eleven (4.4 percent) refusals were recorded but a further 20 percent of respondents supplied information that did not easily fall into the social status range D to A. Rather than lose these respondents, they were given a further three categories and the first, and largest, was the 24 respondents who stated the head of household to be retired, but offered no information on previous occupation. This is a serious omission since the person could have retired on a state pension or that of a Rear Admiral. A small group of respondents were single adults with young children who gave no occupation and whose dependents probably prevented them from working. Finally, 11 respondents declared the head of household to be unemployed and this, at 5.5 percent, was below the average for the district and confirmed the fact that disadvantaged households had not come forward in this survey.

In general, the shopper was not declared as head of household (Table 6.20) and it could reasonably be assumed that the majority of shoppers were women. Neither length of residence (Table 6.21) nor sex of respondent were seen as a key issues at this stage but may emerge as important factors later. For convenience, the responses were seen as being derived from nine areas, (Table 6.22) since the basis of the survey was a census of streets that made up the crucial EDs. It was very frequently the case that one side of the street lay in one ED, whilst the other was in another. EDs AP10, AP11, and AP12 were previously defined as higher income and these supplied 56 percent of responses whereas the lower income EDs AM10, and AM11 supplied 88 responses, 44 percent of the total. It is already clear that, though at Census night 1981 sixty percent of households in ED AM10 were stated as having no car, the rate of no-car households responding to the survey was far lower than this.

DIMENSIONS OF DISADVANTAGE
With a preliminary analysis made of the full list of 43 variables, both 'social' and 'welfare', it was possible to consider which of the techniques proposed (see Chapter three) were appropriate for the analysis of such data. The grouping of 'social' variables had already suggested that 'relative' rather than 'absolute' disadvantage was likely to be dominant. Some of the 'social' constructs were clearly capable of cutting across lines of 'advantage' and 'disadvantage'. Most of the 'welfare' variables also implied that even in the lower income area many shoppers were likely to be mobile. Many could probably adjust their shopping habits to allow access to the family car - for example, by postponing shopping until the evening.

Table 6.19
Frequency distribution of respondents in respect of social class of the head of the household

Social class	Number of respondents	Percentage of respondents
No response	11	5.5
D	14	7.0
C_2	44	22.0
C_1	23	11.5
B	58	29.0
A	11	5.5
Retired – previous not specified	24	12.0
Single person with dependents	5	2.5
Unemployed	11	5.5
TOTALS =	201	100.5

Table 6.20
Frequency distribution of respondents in respect
of respondent also being the head of the household

Respondent also head of household	Number of respondents	Percentage of respondents
Yes	20	10.0
No	180	89.5
No response	1	0.5
TOTALS =	201	100.0

Table 6.21
Frequency distribution of respondents by length of residence

Length of residence	Number of respondents	Percentage of respondents
Under 1 year	13	6.5
1- 5 years	46	23.0
6-10 years	35	17.5
11-20 years	70	35.0
Over 20 years	35	17.5
No response	2	1.0
TOTALS =	201	100.5

Table 6.22
Frequency distribution of respondents by home
location – defined by particular streets within
the enumeration districts

Enumeration districts		Number of respondents	Percentage of respondents
1.	AP10/12	33	16.5
2.	AP10/12	32	16.0
3.	AP12	23	11.5
4.	AP10/11	25	12.5
	Sub-totals	113	56.5
5.	AM10	25	12.5
6.	AM10	19	9.5
7.	AM10/11	18	9.0
8.	AM11	26	13.0
	Sub-totals	88	44.0
	Grand totals	201	100.5

What was now certain was that disadvantage, were it to emerge, would be relative disadvantage. This would preclude any possibility of a Lorenz analysis based on mobility. It had emerged that car ownership levels were uniformly high: it would have been absurd to place along the same continuum the fifteen people without access to a car, plus the vast majority with a car. The distinction between those with a car and those without a car was itself probably the only basis for a real welfare-based dichotomisation of the groups. Furthermore, the crucial distinction between ASDA and Havant Hypermarket was that they were in contrasting locations with one being freestanding, the other near to areas of population. Lorenz, however, is not cast in relation to geographically-fixed points, let alone two of them. Accordingly, Lorenz was finally dismissed as a possible measure of disadvantage in this study. What remained was the conviction that the key distinction in accessibility, and thus 'welfare', was between those with a car and those without. It was decided that considerable attention should be paid to this distinction based on car ownership. Secondly, the patterns of relative disadvantage should be structured through reference to the defined higher income and lower income groups.

IMPLICATIONS FOR RESPONDENTS LACKING A CAR
Only 43 individuals were either unable, or chose, to shop other than by car. This sub-group supplied a wealth of information on their shopping habits that could be drawn upon to emphasise welfare factors. The clearest factor to emerge was the extra amount of time that such shoppers spent travelling to and from their main grocery store. It took some car-owning respondents only five minutes to reach one of the main grocery stores, but more than 40 minutes door-to-door when relying upon the bus. Calculations based on time-distance revealed that no more than 24 respondents in the whole sample were truly disadvantaged. It appeared that the real mobility problems lay with those without a car and who used the bus or walked because they had no other choice. Among the most disadvantaged were two elderly widows living in the higher income area and who were forced to rely upon a very infrequent bus service. The other 22 disadvantaged individuals were drawn from the lower income area which attests to the validity of sampling from those areas.

What emerged most forcefully from the detailed examination of shopping habits was that the clearest measure of welfare for those who suffered disadvantage in their shopping was the availability of and frequency of bus services. The one individual defined as most disadvantaged with respect to shopping was an elderly lady in the higher income area who was dependent upon the bus to reach her nearest foodstore - Tesco, Waterlooville.

She remarked specifically upon the infrequency of the service to her area and observed that on occasion the bus failed to appear at all. This was clearly stressful for one so frail and so dependent upon public transport. It was evident that further detail on bus provision prevailing at the time of survey was needed. Accordingly, Figure 6.3 provides this information by showing all local bus services and their frequency. No statistical analysis was required to confirm how much better served was ASDA Waterlooville than Havant Hypermarket. ASDA was reached by 135 scheduled daily bus services as compared with just 55 at Havant Hypermarket. It was also abundantly clear that the bus company wisely directed its services through the areas of lowest car ownership. Ironically, this served to emphasise the disadvantage of those less mobile individuals who were located in areas of generally high car ownership. The bus route policy is clearly one that compensates, at least in part, for general disadvantage. In aggregate terms, the lowerstatus local authority areas genuinely need the bus services and are most inclined to support them.

Examination of comments on store accessibility offered during the survey in chapter four revealed that seven specifically related to ASDA's easier accessibility by bus, whilst many others implied such an advantage. This seemed to imply that many people saw mobility as a key issue. 1981 census data were correlated to test for this and it emerged that the percentage of local authority tenants in an area correlated strongly with the percentage without a car ($rs = +0.822$, p <0.01). Correlating percentage local authority households with percent unemployed gave a further highly significant result ($rs = +0.807$, $p < 0.01$). The corollary of this was that the correlation between the percentage of owner-occupied households and the percentage owning two or more cars was also highly significant ($rs = +0.685$, $p < 0.05$). When owner occupation was correlated with unemployment this revealed a highly significant inverse relationship ($rs = -0.796$, $p < 0.05$). Clearly, the general policy of selecting among the local authority areas when seeking those most likely to suffer relative disadvantage was justified (as was the routing policy of the bus company). Figure 6.3 perhaps demonstrates more clearly than any other single piece of evidence how superior is the location of ASDA as compared with Havant Hypermarket when the welfare demands of lower income individuals is the prime concern.

LORENZ REFORMULATED
The specific detail on shopping thus far obtained pointed to the fact that very few respondents were genuinely deprived and that probably none suffered absolute disadvantage. The aggregate

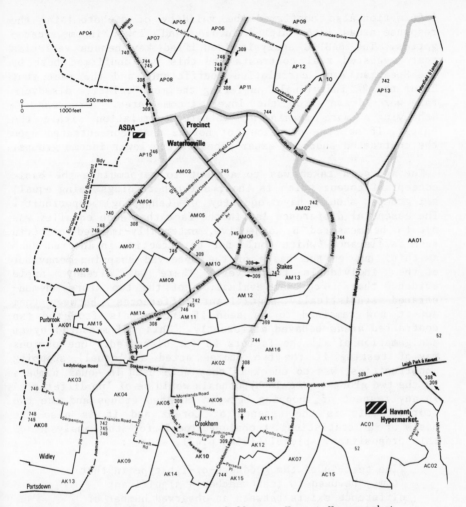

Daily service frequency 8.30am to 8.30pm at Havant Hypermarket

Route	No. of Buses
52	17
308/309	38

Daily service frequency 8.30am to 8.30pm at Waterlooville Precinct

Route	No. of Buses
740/744	45
748/749	26
742/746	11
745	15
308/309	38

Figure 6.3 Frequency of bus services to vicinity of ASDA, Waterlooville, and Havant Hypermarket, and passing through selected enumeration districts.

information also confirmed the validity of dichotomising the response areas into higher income and lower income categories. The SASPAC analysis identified key census variables that suggested real contrasts and this was confirmed both by the Spearman Rank correlation coefficients and the fact that 22 of the 24 individuals suffering the most relative disadvantage were drawn from the lower income area. Progress on achieving a more meaningful welfare formulation within the spirit, if not the practice, of Lorenz next concentrated upon the contrasted shopping experiences of the lower income groups.

The approach taken was to attempt to reformulate the basic concept of Lorenz which is that, all other things being equal, all groups should have equality of (shopping) opportunity. The essential difference lay in the fact that such equality was not to be measured by objective, externally-imposed criteria such as distance (which could not be effective in an area such as this) but on the basis of the observed shopping behaviour of the individuals themselves. There was already ample evidence that perceptual evaluation of the two stores demonstrated statistically significant differences between them and it now remained to be seen if individuals from the two contrasted areas behaved differently. This was measured by an amalgamation of all the factors so far discussed. One obvious way of testing if the two stores acted as 'equal' shopping opportunities, was to check if they were used in equal numbers by the two groups. A null hypothesis would be of 'no difference' in any respect of shopping between the two groups and the two stores. This is the essence of Lorenz and it is also the basis of a statistical technique ideal for the analysis of this proposition. Siegel (1956, p.43), states:

> "The test is of the goodness-of-fit type in that
> it may be used to test whether a significant
> difference exists between an observed number of
> objects or responses falling in each category
> and an expected number based on the null hypothesis."

This was exactly the requirement, since it was hypothesised that the two contrasting groups, (which would have lain at opposite ends of a Lorenz axis) would differ in their observed usage of the two stores.

All variables, both those on 'social' aspects of shopping and the 'welfare' variables, were subjected to two-sample χ^2 analysis. The two sample areas taken were those already defined as higher income and lower income. In many cases the calculations were analysed in the form of 'reduced' matrices wherever the 'full' matrices infringed the requirements of the model. This procedure was followed, for example, with the variable 'shopping for groceries is usually enjoyable'. There were so few responses in category 5 'very strongly agree', that x^2 could not be adopted directly. Instead, the two categories representing negative responses were collapsed into one. With the same procedure applied to the positive responses, x^2 could be used. Thus, in cell 1 of the 'reduced' matrix, a value of 49 for the higher income group was made up of nine responses indicating very strong disagreement and 40 indicating slight disagreement. The variables relating to social factors in shopping were included in this analysis specifically in order to reveal which of them would split on welfare grounds and which would transcend welfare constraints.

THE LOWER INCOME AND HIGHER INCOME GROUPS COMPARED – THE 'SOCIAL' VARIABLES

Attention was first turned to those variables where a statistically significant difference emerged (Table 6.23). In this table, an asterisk is used to denote that certain calculations were based upon the 'reduced' matrix as outlined above and in these instances the critical values of x^2 were 3.84 and 6.64 for 5 percent and 1 percent significance respectively. Where it was possible to use the full 5-cell matrix, the critical values were 9.49 and 13.28 for 5 percent and 1 percent significance respectively. Table 6.24 shows the variables where a significant difference was not obtained.

The first variable to demonstrate a statistically significant difference between the higher income and lower income groups was that contrasting good shops and good parking (x^2 = 10.38, df = 4, p < 0.05). x^2 cannot be partialled, but the general conclusion appeared to be that those from the higher income area were not likely to rate parking more highly than good shops. This may seem a little unusual given the higher car ownership figures for this area but there were two possible explanations. One was that responses to this variable may have involved a 'halo effect'. The second was that the question was perhaps somewhat simplistic in that it forced a choice between parking and good shops. Many shoppers may not have had to make that choice since both ASDA and Havant Hypermarket provided good new shopping whilst also providing good parking. Higher income respondents probably required both good shops and good parking but rated the former more highly when forced to choose. With regard to shopping being a nuisance (x^2 = 4.17, df = 1, p < 0.05), the lower income groups tended to find shopping more of a nuisance. It may be that their lower incomes forced them to use stores where shopping was more of a chore – or that they could not reach the better shops. Note, too, that the question related to shopping *per se*, rather

Table 6.23
'Social aspects of shopping' variables demonstrating
a significant difference between higher income and
lower income groups under χ^2 analysis

Variable number	Variable Description
3	Given a choice between good shops and good parking facilities, I would choose to shop where there is better parking
* 5	I find shopping is a nuisance and try to get it done as quickly as possible
* 6	I find shopping for my groceries very tiring
9	The convenience of local shops is worth the extra it can cost
*14	I don't mind going out of my way to get to better shops
*15	I find the staff more friendly in small shops
*18	I would prefer to do all my shopping just once a week
*21	I prefer to shop at the 'small man' type of shop
*22	I always try to buy good quality food – even if prices are higher

* Based on reduced matrix

(Significance at 5 per cent)

Table 6.24
'Social aspects of shopping' variables not
demonstrating a significant difference between
higher income and lower income groups under χ^2
analysis

Variable number	Variable Description
1	Shopping for groceries is usually enjoyable
2	I like shopping because it gets me out of the house
4	I usually do my grocery shopping on a journey when I do errands or other shopping
7	I usually do a lot of comparing of prices for ordinary food shopping
8	When I am shopping I am usually in a hurry
10	I usually try hard to look for bargains
11	Going grocery shopping gives you the chance to meet friends and acquaintances
12	Getting shopping done quickly is very important to me
13	I try to avoid walking for more than five minutes with a bag of shopping
16	When it comes to buying food, price is not important to me
17	Chain stores and supermarkets make for better grocery shopping all round
19	There's not much difference between shops these days
20	The way a person shops for the household groceries is a good indication of how capable they are all round

than food shopping alone, and the higher income groups probably had more of their surplus income to spend on comparison goods where shopping can, indeed, be more enjoyable. With respect to shopping being tiring ($x^2 = 5.15$, df = 1, p < 0.05), results showed that more of those from the lower income area agreed with this proposition. Since three times as many of them were forced to rely on transport other than the car this was hardly surprising.

An interesting finding was that local shops, ($x^2 = 8.2$, df = 1, p < 0.01) were far more attractive to respondents from the higher income areas and it was worthwhile to consider this in detail. It may be that, for some of these people, Waitrose was probably the nearest, *i.e.* 'local' shop - and prices there were generally higher. The other side of this argument was made at the very start of this study: that lower income residents, here seen as most disadvantaged, do not wish to pay more than necessary for groceries. If they are at all mobile they wish to reach a large, cut-price grocery outlet. To suggest that such people can always find satisfactory grocery shops even when large stores are beyond their reach is simply not acceptable. They themselves expressed this by repudiating the suggestion that it was worthwhile to pay more. The above points have something of a corollary with respect to 'using better shops' (with a significant $x^2 = 5.56$, df = 1, p < 0.05) where, as a group, it was generally the more mobile higher income shoppers who were prepared to go out of their way to reach better shops. Such groups may also have been prone to notice the 'halo effect' which is always a problem with variables such as this. The higher income group claimed ($x^2 = 4.2$, df = 1, p < 0.05) to be more likely to find the staff more friendly in small shops, and yet again the interpretation came down to what one defined as 'small'. The group may have been referring to small, expensive, 'specialised' shops which previous studies had shown upper income groups to use, rather than the 'small man' type of shop so generally disliked when presented as an attitudinal variable.

Those from the higher income area were less likely ($x^2 = 8.87$, df = 1, p < 0.01) to 'prefer to do shopping just once a week', but it should be noted that the vast majority of all respondents did prefer this mode of shopping. All but 13 shoppers disliked the 'small man' type of shop but the split among them was sufficiently uneven as to confirm that the people from the lower income area did not wish to shop at the more expensive small shop ($x^2 = 4.83$, df = 1, p < 0.05). Predictably, the advantaged groups claimed to buy food for quality rather than price and they were best equipped to do so ($x^2 = 17.92$, df = 1, p < 0.01).

This concluded the analysis of the variables relating to 'social' aspects of shopping. It may be that these variables can form the basis for identifying 'shopper types'. The results from the principal components analysis seemed to provide evidence for such a typology. Production of such a typology, is however, not the primary purpose of this work. The important variables are the eight which showed differences between respondents from the higher income and the lower income areas. In part, expected differences did emerge, but such social variables mostly serve to illustrate what a complex process shopping is. One possible explanation for the pattern of results was that lower income groups may have had a tendency to value grocery shopping more highly as a part of their routine. This overall stance would go some considerable way to explaining the pattern of results which did throw up some apparent inconsistencies. At the same time, any variable that hinted at higher grocery prices was rejected by the disadvantaged groups and access to low prices emerged as vital for them. Whatever the behavioural influences on one's attitudes to shopping, the position taken here echoes that of Hudson (1980) that it is constraint rather than choice that is paramount.

COMPARISON OF 'WELFARE' VARIABLES

The emphasis on constraint made it essential to study closely the 'main store used'. ASDA had scored consistently strongly on welfare variables in Chapter five, whilst Havant Hypermarket scored very well on non-welfare variables. It was important to see the extent to which the two groups used the two stores. Table 6.25 presents the direct χ^2 comparison (χ^2 = 2.18, df = 1, p > 0.05) and no significant difference was revealed. Slightly more of the lower income group used ASDA, slightly more of the higher income group used Havant Hypermarket. Yet, overall, both groups tended to use ASDA far more than Havant Hypermarket and so overall there was no significant difference. Figure 6.4 emphasises this by presenting those households choosing either ASDA or Havant Hypermarket and ignoring all other stated shops, whilst Figure 6.5 presents the fuller picture. It is probable that the location of ASDA was so advantageous that this overrode other considerations for both groups. Certainly, in this area of roughly equal general accessibility, there was no suggestion of an equal split of patronage - ASDA was the clear winner for both groups. This testifies to the advantages of the district centre location.

When the results for Tesco were added, the picture changed since more lower income respondents entered the sample. This emphasised more forcefully the dependence of lower income respondents upon the district centre. It was also the case

137

Table 6.25
Frequency distribution of respondents by usage
of ASDA, Waterlooville, or Havant Hypermarket
for the two contrasted groups

Source area	Store stated as used	
	ASDA, Waterlooville	Havant Hypermarket
Total numbers of patrons from the higher income area	47	18
Total numbers of patrons from the lower income area	50	10

χ^2 Analysis : Calculated χ^2 = 2.18, df = 1, p > 0.05

Shoppers using:-

● ASDA
○ Havant Hypermarket

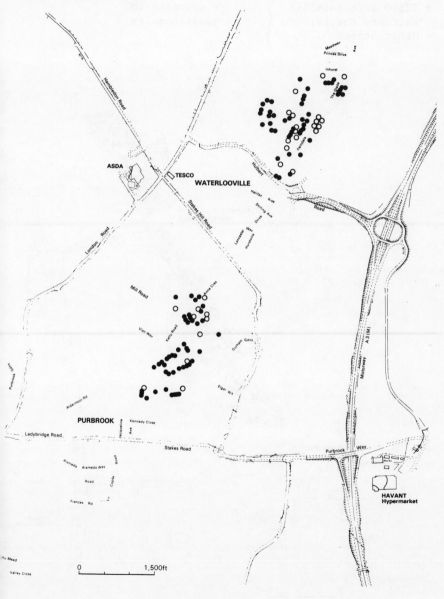

Figure 6.4 Home locations of households using either ASDA,
Waterlooville, or Havant Hypermarket

Shoppers using:-

◆ ASDA
· Havant Hypermarket
● TESCO Waterlooville   Householders
- Waitrose Cowplain   responding to
· Other Stores   questionnaire

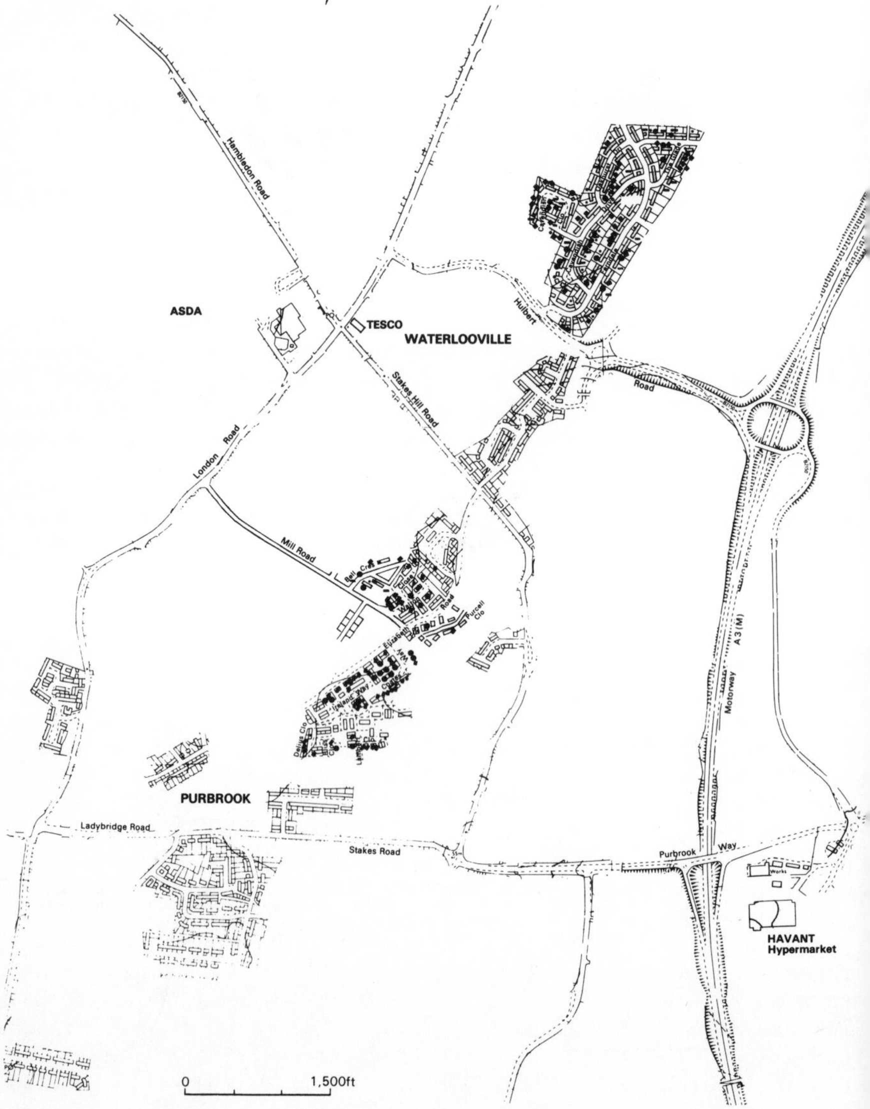

Figure 6.5 Home locations of households using all stores
in the study area

140

that five of the six residents of the higher income area experiencing most difficulty with shopping, used Tesco - the store physically nearest to them. Four walked, one went by bus, and so, at this level of resolution, the results picked out the less advantaged shoppers within the higher income areas. Expanding the matrix again to include the upmarket Waitrose store increased the significance of the test statistic (X^2 = 25.1, df = 3, p < 0.01) as shown in Table 6.26. Twenty-five advantaged and only two disadvantaged shoppers used Waitrose, but this is moving further out of the realms of 'equal accessibility'. Waitrose was markedly nearer to the higher income area, but this table did begin to point to a link between 'store image' and 'shopper status' which is an obvious area for future research.

SUMMARY OF WELFARE RESULTS
The research presented in this section has confirmed that ASDA is greatly preferred by those in the area of spatial indifference between the stores and that aspects of personal preference added a complicating dimension to this. Table 6.27 demonstrates how the higher income and lower income groups contrasted in respect of the welfare variables and this confirmed the validity of taking the two groupings despite clear evidence that the higher income area contained some disadvantaged individuals. The significant test statistic for 'mode of transport' showed that far more respondents from the lower income area had to walk to their grocery store. There was a great difference in car ownership patterns between the groups (χ^2 = 51.79, df = 3, p < 0.01) and only nine respondents from the lower income area owned more than two cars, whilst 65 of those from the higher income area did so. Car availability also demonstrated significant differences, since 91 of the higher income group had a car available for shopping at all times as compared with only 36 of the lower income group. This was compounded by results on possession of a driving licence where members of the higher income group were markedly more likely to have a licence. This latter factor emerged despite the fact that the higher income area tended to have generally older residents, yet it is usually younger people who presently tend to have driving licences.

No significant difference between the two groups emerged with respect to time of day for shopping. There was no major reason to expect such a difference and, had one emerged, it might have indicated some further complicating factor with respect to the two groups. Though giving a significant result, the test statistic in 'stores too far to reach' (χ^2 = 16.02, df = 1, p < 0.05) added little to the simple observation already made that the higher income groups seemed to perceive a form of relative disadvantage with respect to the lack of a nearby Sainsbury outlet.

Table 6.26
Frequency distribution of respondents using ASDA and Tesco, Waterlooville, Havant Hypermarket and Waitrose Havant

Source area	Store used			
	ASDA, Waterlooville	Tesco Waterlooville	Havant Hypermarket	Waitrose Havant
Total numbers of patrons from the higher income area	47	18	14	25
Total numbers of patrons from the lower income area	50	10	24	2

χ^2 Analysis : Calculated χ^2 = 25.10, df = 3, p < 0.05

Table 6.27
Resumé of χ^2 comparison of higher income and lower income groups with regard to variables on constraints to shopping

Variable name	χ^2 Calculated	Critical value at $p < 0.05$	Statistically significant differences between higher income and lower income groups
Mode of transport	16.64	3.84	Yes
Car ownership	51.79	7.82	Yes
Car availability	23.81	3.84	Yes
Posession of car licence	16.33	3.84	Yes
Time of day when shopping done	1.30	5.99	No
Stores stated as too far	16.00	3.84	Yes
Children in household	41.94	7.82	Yes
Children under 5	5.77	3.84	Yes
Pensioners in household	26.96	5.99	Yes
Age of shopper	56.65	9.49	Yes
Does shopper also work?	3.50	3.84	No
Full or part-time	0.50	3.84	No
Status of head of household	136.15	7.82	Yes
Social status	110.34	5.99	Yes
Shopper as head of household	0.38	3.84	No
Length of residence	13.14	9.49	Yes

Attention was next turned to household characteristics and these confirmed that the lower income households tended to have higher numbers of children present. This was hardly surprising since one of the keys to access to Local Authority housing is to have at least one or two children. This inevitably fed on to the numbers of children aged less than five found to be present. Little evidence had so far emerged on the difficulties of shopping with children and, indeed, mobility seemed to be the only major welfare problem and this was not necessarily related to age. A high percentage of pensioners contacted seemed to be very mobile and to be able to use a car. It was by no means certain that the presence of pensioners necessarily implied shopping disadvantages. The 'impact study' results showed clearly that persons in the pensioner age groups were well represented at both stores and especially at Havant Hyper-market. Mention has already been made of the differences in age profiles with respect to holding a driving licence and, in clear interrelationship with the last three variables also, it was confirmed that a statistically significant difference between the stores emerged with respect to age of shopper. There was no significant difference between the groups with respect to the likelihood of the shopper working (which may be read as female employment) though there was a tendency for more individuals in the advantaged area to hold a job. What the figures did confirm was the high level of female employment in the area – at least equivalent to the national average.

Since the groups were dichotomised as lower income and higher income because of their tenure and other census characteristics, it would be unfortunate if the samples did not vary in terms of status of head of household. In fact, a significant test statistic of 136.15 emerged and note should be made that all the unemployed were drawn from the lower income area and all the A, B, group respondents (69 in all) were drawn from the higher income area. When attention was focussed on estimated social class groupings and the three *ad hoc* groupings omitted, then a significant difference emerged (χ^2 = 110.34, df = 2, p < 0.05) with, for example, all the D group respondents being found in the lower income area. The penultimate variable showed that there was no difference between the areas in respect of the shopper being head of household and the figures imply that residents of both areas saw this as women's work. A final difference emerged in respect of length of residence, largely due to the greater numbers of higher income respondents who had lived in the area more than 20 years. The Local Authority estate was built only some 20 years ago so residents could not have lived in the area as long as those in the private sector.

OVERALL CONCLUSIONS FROM ANALYSIS OF WELFARE-RELATED VARIABLES
The variables on social factors of shopping did not contribute greatly to the overall understanding of welfare except in that those from the lower income area reacted strongly to any variable related to price. However, the two groups did begin to demonstrate some differences in behaviour patterns that could be related to store accessibility, always bearing in mind that ASDA dominated as chosen grocery store. It must also be noted that as disadvantage was probed more deeply, the most severe cases of relative disadvantage did not coincide exclusively with the lower income areas; a point made earlier. Of the 24 individuals most disadvantaged in respect of shopping, the two living in the higher income area were the most disadvantaged shoppers found in the whole study.

There remained two contrasting ways in which the welfare dimension of shopping could be further illuminated and one of these involved delving further into the data provided by the two groups. Some of the complexities of the interrelationships were disentangled by the cross-tabulation of variables and this took the form of two-way or three-way cross-tabulations. The second approach was to examine more closely the statements made on shopping by individuals when completing their questionnaires.

TWO-WAY CROSS-TABULATION
In the first of these approaches, 72 two-way tabulations were attempted, many of which were aimed at refining the details of group accessibility patterns. It was revealed, for example, that only one 'shopper' of those living in sample households with three cars or more had no licence. The most common pattern was to be a licence-holder living in a household with one car. This detailed level of analysis confirmed what had earlier been surmised: that licence-holding in the higher income areas held up well with age and that the elderly were generally mobile. The majority of people over the age of 60 had a driving licence, which was the reverse of the pattern for the under-30 group. Licence-holding was a distinctive characteristic of the higher income area and of the upper status groups who lived there. 91 percent of A group respondents possessed a licence compared with only 50 percent of D group respondents and 40 percent of those recorded as unemployed. It was discovered that in one ED in the higher income area, only four percent of respondents had no driving licence whereas in one lower income ED the figure was 55 percent. This cross-tabulation also served to confirm the way in which choosing two maximally-contrasted groups resulted in an under-representation of the middle social status (C1) category since only 23 responses came from this group, despite the fact that it was well represented in the general area.

145

When attention was turned to the usage of stores, cross-tabulation revealed ASDA and Tesco to be attractive to the under-30 age group. This group had already been seen to have the lowest levels of car ownership and was essentially drawn from the Local Authority area. The tabulation thus emphasised both accessibility and price considerations. Out of 26 respondents in the youngest age category, 17 shopped at ASDA, eight at Tesco and just one at Havant Hypermarket. A virtually identical pattern emerged with respect to the shopping habits of the D Social Status group; whereas the modal status group of those shopping at Waitrose was the B category. It was again emphasised that the less mobile and the less wealthy were attracted — or constrained — to shop at the stores in the nearby Waterlooville district centre.

It was felt that some cross-tabulation of the attitudinal variables would also add to the welfare perspective. It emerged (as one could earlier only surmise) that car-owners were better placed than pedestrians to avoid the problem of carrying heavy bags. 110 respondents who shopped by car agreed that they tried to avoid walking with heavy bags, as opposed to only nine who shopped on foot.

This attitudinal variable was every bit as revealing in a welfare context as any of the factual pieces of data gathered on shopper characteristics. Families with three cars were the only ones where a majority of respondents did not see shopping as a nuisance — a pattern exactly reproduced with respect to finding shopping to be tiring.

Arguments in favour of the district centre as the optimal location for shops were reinforced when the question on licence-holding was cross-tabulated with the question on shopping for groceries in conjunction with other errands. Of 132 licence-holders only 60 (45 percent) were inclined to do other errands on a grocery trip whereas of the 61 non-licence-holders 38 (62 percent) were inclined to do other errands. It was further possible to confirm the tendency for the car-owning groups to go out of their way to better shops and the B Social class group were particularly likely to do this. On the other hand, as expected, the D Social class group and the unemployed were particularly inclined to seek bargains and this added further emphasis to the importance for such groups of cheap prices. Finally, with respect to the purely social role of shopping, it appeared that the households with lower levels of car ownership were more likely to see shopping as a measure of being 'capable all round'. This may simply follow from the fact that they were constrained to spend more of their time shopping. Those without children were more likely to value the role of shopping - presumably those with children had other concerns.

THREE-WAY CROSS-TABULATION
The two-way cross-tabulations still left considerable complexity unresolved and yet, because of large numbers of empty cells in the matrices, the data did not lend themselves to further multivariate analysis. A compromise was to apply three-way cross-tabulation where two variables could be compared whilst a third was held constant. This produced a finer categorisation of which individuals were advantaged and which were disadvantaged in respect of car ownership and licence-holding, both of which were crucial to shopping. For example, it had been shown that licence-holding held up well with age and suggested a mobile elderly population. Three -way tabulation showed that the pattern of licence-holding among the older groups was almost exclusively a phenomenon of the higher income area. It revealed that 46 individuals over the age of 50 had a licence but 41 of these lived in the higher income area. When attention was paid to those over 60 it emerged, that of 17 with a licence, 16 lived in the higher income area. It was also revealed that 112 individuals had both a licence and a car always available for shopping and these were surely the most advantaged respondents.

Car availability led to morning shopping trips - by far the preferred time for those whose trips were in no way constrained. The detail of the analysis was such that three individuals could be identified who could have used a car to shop but actually went on foot. The relationship between social status and car ownership was confirmed by the fact that in A and B status households it was most likely that every adult would have a car. It was also shown that, whatever the status of the household, if there was no car present then the only stores used were ASDA and Tesco, both of which are located in Water-looville district centre. This was crucial confirmation of the impression conveyed in the two-way cross-tabulation that the less mobile shopper used the district centre.

Another point brought out more clearly by cross-tabulation was the relationship between age of respondent and preferred store since it was now possible to control for the effects of social status. In the D social status group two of the youngest shoppers used ASDA, one used Tesco and the figures for the C2 group were eight and five respectively. Again it was seen that the district centre was favoured by the less mobile younger shopper who was also in the lower social status groupings.

147

Subsequent 3-way tabulations were focussed on the attitudinal variables and showed that there was general agreement among all groups (disaggregated by mode of transport) that grocery shopping indicated 'capability'. However, those who shopped on foot were less likely to find enjoyment in grocery shopping. Generally there was disagreement that shopping 'gets one out of the house' or offered 'a chance to meet friends' except among the one-parent 'solo' households, where there was some agreement that this was the case. The desire for companionship among this group may have caused them to see shopping as an opportunity for social interaction. It has several times been emphasised how the less mobile use the shopping trip to do other errands and the three-way tabulation also clarified this. The store demonstrating the least likelihood of this happening was Havant Hypermarket where only a third of respondents claimed to also take on other errands. The strongest tendency for doing other errands was shown by Tesco shoppers, using the store in the very centre of Waterlooville. This pattern involving Tesco and other errands applied whatever the mode of transport and was especially prevalent among car-users. This led to the assumption that Tesco – with the worst parking of all the major stores – attracted the car-borne shopper who already had other business in the centre.

Whichever store was under scrutiny, when those who shopped on foot or by bus were analysed, the tendency was for them to value the opportunity to undertake errands on the shopping trip. It was also shown that shoppers who worked were markedly more likely to state that they were in a hurry whatever age group was concerned. Unemployment appeared to be the main determinant of seeing shopping as a sign of 'capability'. It may be that successful shopping offered the unemployed at least some opportunity to demonstrate that they were capable individuals. Alternatively it may have been that shopping as cheaply as possible was really important to the household budget of the unemployed.

SHOPPER STATEMENTS
The final piece of evidence on welfare aspects of shopping was the list of freely-elicited statements. It is well known that such lists are biased in favour of those who are best able to express themselves and thus they favour the better-educated respondent. What was clear, however, was that if a person offered a statement then it was almost certain to be very relevant to her, or his, shopping experience. It represented a distillation of all the influences so far listed into simple expressions of satisfaction or dissatisfaction. Statements stood as discrete pieces of information and defied generalisations even if some complex content analysis was attempted.

Whilst, for example, seventeen out of the 51 responses made some reference to convenience and six made some reference to being in a hurry, the greatest information was gained from treating the statements as distinct entities. The shopping experience of the elderly lady in the higher income area was conveyed far more directly by her statement than by any disaggregation of social or welfare variables. It also emerged from the statements that shopping with small children was more of an ordeal than had been conveyed by the data tabulations. The fact that very few people responded to a particular question did not diminish the importance of that issue for those who did. It may be that for more than half of the sample there were no difficulties whatsoever in easily reaching a satisfactory store and conveying home the goods. The essence of a welfare formulation was to seek out those who were disadvantaged and to attempt to discover ways in which matters might be improved.

The women with babies were a case in point and their problems seemed to focus on the changing and feeding facilities which some large stores are now beginning to provide. Indeed, only large stores can possibly find the space for feeding and changing rooms. There will be a genuine case of relative disadvantage towards mothers with babies if large stores, with the facilities they want, are placed in inaccessible locations. 'Help the Aged' have listed factors such as toilets and sloping ramps that enable the elderly to enjoy shopping and yet again these are best provided by large new stores.

CONCLUSIONS
This extensive chapter on welfare formulations has demonstrated quite clearly that relative disadvantage is essentially intuitive and experiential. The Lorenz approach could not be applied to this type of situation but the data tabulations allowed the possibility of a χ^2 approach that was entirely within the spirit of Lorenz. χ^2 demonstrated real differences in the practicalities of shopping as experienced by the higher income and lower income groups and supplemented this with some evidence on the importance of social aspects of shopping.

The district centre was an important focus of the bus routes upon which many lower income individuals were constrained to depend. Evidence emerged that such groups made effective use of their time and money by taking on other errands on the shopping trip. Indeed, that tendency may have been underestimated since there was no direct inspection of shopping diaries and it is known that people shop on far more trips than those stated as begun for the primary purpose of shopping. Where shops were near a post office, a library, or a bank, visits to those facilities were possible as an adjunct to the shopping trip - and vice-versa. On the other hand, the higher income shopper had the freedom to eschew the nearest outlet. Relative disadvantage for such people in this area could be cast only in terms of poor accessibility to a Sainsburys store. The most striking fact of all was that ASDA, hypothesised as being in the better location, was also the store that respondents from both groups tended to choose as their preferred store.

It was evident that, even in suburban southern England, genuine differences in the shopping experience of contrasted social groups did emerge and could be measured statistically. Whilst Pareto and Lorenz analyses could not be used, χ^2 testing pointed to demonstrable differences in shopping experience that proved that the less mobile, less advantaged, groups were constrained to shop in the district centre. In such a centre they found a large supermarket, or superstore, that offered them the cheap prices they sought. Small, local, shops may be convenient but they were not seen as cheap. Waterlooville seemed to be an attractive place for the disadvantaged to shop in that they had both an ASDA superstore and a Tesco supermarket readily accessible by public transport. It is essential to discover how the placement of the superstore came about, and what the likelihood is that other disadvantaged groups near other district centres will gain similar shopping opportunities. The following final chapter discusses the planning dimensions of the type of superstore location that has now clearly been demonstrated as having welfare advantages.

7 Conclusions and policy prescriptions

INTRODUCTION
This final chapter has two aims, one is to present a summary of the welfare findings from the work as a whole and the other is to put forward some policy prescriptions for food retailing. The policy suggestions relate exclusively to food retailing since this sector alone has been subject to empirical investigation in this study. Nevertheless, it is the sector that carries with it the greatest implications for consumer welfare. Firstly, however, it is necessary to summarise exactly what the empirical research has demonstrated in respect of large-scale foodstores.

RESULTS
The research reported in this study has shown that statistically significant differences exist in the ability of higher income groups and lower income groups to overcome the frictional effects of distance to shopping. These findings emerged despite the fact that the study area was spatially restricted and also in a part of the affluent suburban south east of England. Residents in an area of Local Authority housing were shown to have disproportionately lower levels of mobility and lower car ownership figures. They were also less likely to hold a driving licence. Only the specific problems of individuals who are elderly and immobile failed to be revealed by this choice of study area. At the same time, certain less advantaged individuals were found to be living in the higher

income study area that was selected as a contrast to the Local
Authority area. In the context of ASDA, Waterlooville and
Havant Hypermarket, real welfare-related differences emerged.
As predicted, the characteristics of the clientele interviewed
at the two stores showed marked differences. The ASDA store
appealed more to shoppers wishing, or constrained, to shop on
foot or by bus. Perceptual evaluation of the two stores based
on respondents in the zone of spatial indifference confirmed
this distinction. Neither store was in an area provided with
major employment opportunities but, this apart, ASDA gained
better evaluations with regard to the locational factors under
study. This was confirmed by a series of statements drawn
from respondents. The bulk of these related to the locational
advantage of the district-centre ASDA store. At the same
time, Havant Hypermarket, generally considered to be a particularly good example of the hypermarket format, scored exception-
ally well on the non-locational factors.

Analysis involving the estimation of shopper attitudes did
not show major differences emerging when the results were
dichotomised on a welfare basis. Only eight from 22 such
variables revealed a significant statistical difference when
contrasted in this way. It may, however, be the case that
these attitudinal variables are capable of identifying shopper
group 'types' that cut across welfare boundaries. The key
finding to emerge from the second major questionnaire survey
undertaken was that the locationally-superior ASDA store dominated the area of spatial indifference between the two stores.
Although they are sufficiently similar that they act as mutual
intervening opportunities for shoppers prepared to travel
long distances to shop, when they are in direct competition
the present evidence is that ASDA is preferred. Attention
should be paid here to the results derived from the analysis
of further shoppers' statements for these confirm both the
complexity of shopping and the key factor of location. In
conclusion, then, the ASDA store fared markedly better on
most welfare-based measures. Consumers in the zone of spatial
indifference confirmed this by offering their patronage to
ASDA.

Historically, the debate on large foodstores has been conducted at a hypothetical level. It has been seen that a number
of commentators for example, Schiller (1979), have favoured,
largely on grounds of relief of congestion, a large-scale
decanting of grocery stores to the urban fringe. Others,
including many Hampshire planners, have maintained that all
retailing should be located in established centres often using
the argument that the countryside should not be infringed.
Under the British planning system some retailing has subur-

banised itself largely on an *ad hoc* basis. Often this has been through recourse to an appeal to the Minister of State of the Department of the Environment. The position is, therefore, that no level of planning authority can make a watertight, enforceable plan that will apply effectively in all situations. Given the lack of flexibility and foresight in many plans, this is probably to be welcomed. The end-product has been a system that has generally opposed hypermarket developments, but has often proved powerless to stop them. Nevertheless, as Hallsworth (1985c) has shown, far fewer hypermarkets than superstores have come to be developed.

The essential point about the present study is that it has provided empirical evidence on the relative merits of hypermarkets and superstores. This was facilitated by the ideal coincidence, in the same catchment area, of archetypal hypermarket and superstore outlets. Previous studies on such a theme have largely been forced to simulate the possible effects of large stores. It was especially advantageous here to have two stores that were in such close proximity, faced with contrasting planning experiences and yet opened within such a short space of time of one another. It is not easy to imagine that any other area demonstrates quite such an ideal combination of circumstances for the cross-comparison of stores. This does, of course, imply that the approach was strongly idiographic, but the arguments of Thorpe (1978) that retail studies are inevitably place-specific was borne in mind from the outset. The approach has been sufficiently standardised and general to allow a degree of generalisation from an admittedly particular set of circumstances.

GENERAL IMPLICATIONS OF THE RESULTS
In this section the implications of the above evidence for retail foodstore development are considered. Retailers have to act in the interests of their market share whilst planners, on the other hand, act at various levels; local, regional and national. Within Hampshire, the County level of planning is unlikely to shift from a position of urban containment and preference for district centres. However, there is substantial evidence that many local district councils are not averse to certain types of freestanding out-of-town stores. In many cases there is a substantial financial attraction in disposing of peripheral council-owned sites for development by out-of-town DIY 'sheds'.

One argument used is that DIY sheds generate far less traffic than superstores but have, nevertheless, large space requirements that are difficult to accommodate in towns. DIY sheds have met with little opposition, even at local level, yet the converse argument is that their removal does little to aid in-centre traffic congestion and they are just as visually intrusive as superstores. There is assumed to be less of a welfare implication for consumers in the leakage of these types of goods to out-of-town locations. The major test may come when permission is sought to convert such a 'shed' to food sales; though it must be noted that DOE circular 1/85 notes that planners may specify conditions to prevent this from happening.

The paramount level of planning control is at the national level. That there has been no updating of Development Control Policy Note 13 since 1977, when a Labour government was in power, cannot be taken as evidence that there has been no change of attitude within the Department of the Environment. One likely reason why DIY 'sheds' face such little local opposition is that, since traffic grounds are so weak, opponents would be almost certain to lose any appeal to the Department of the Environment. Though circular 1/85, noted above, allows steps to be taken to prevent use changes from DIY to food, it is nevertheless a document designed to speed planning permission by curtailing planners' rights to impose conditions upon developers. No less than 14 sets of conditions are outlined which, by implication, had been imposed in the past and should not be imposed in future. The general view now being taken is that any form of development is permissible provided that it does not threaten the viability of whole town centres. This is clearly a liberalising of attitude that is a major boost to the prospects for decentralised retailing. It would clearly, too, bring exaggerated conflict with the planning 'ethos' of a County such as Hampshire. Policy makers, then, cannot be taken as a whole; some might be receptive to welfare-based criteria, others, evidently, would not.

PROSPECTS FOR DISTRICT CENTRES
The preferred position might be to propose some 'middle ground' that recognises both past failings and present reality. Planners, often restricted by the very system within which they operate, have often been less than far-sighted in their proposals. The major planning acts of 1947 and 1968 gave an opportunity, readily grasped, for intense conservatism motivated by ideas of conservation, containment and control. The end-product has been continual conflict with retailers anxious to develop store formats that would lead to greater profits and greater efficiency and, it must be stated, lower prices – a key welfare criterion. Probably the most direct consequence of planning, often lamented by Hall (see especially Hall *et al* 1973), has been the creation of a restricted and expensive land market.

There can be no doubt that to place blanket restrictions on superstore development by insisting that they only locate in district centres implies a penalty in the form of high land prices upon the compliant superstore operator. It would be reasonable to assume, for example, that ASDA have found expansion to be easy as a result of their cooperation with planners but that they face two possible penalties if the ground rules are changed from those above by a Secretary of State adopting a very liberal attitude in respect of future store applications. One is that they have been forced to pay high land prices for centrally-located stores and they might now come to face rivals trading from more cost-effective peripheral sites. Secondly, whilst ASDA, Waterlooville has been shown to be a preferred location even for the mobile, there must be other situations where an existing superstore could be undercut by a peripheral hypermarket more accessible to the wealthier sectors of the community. This would seem to be a heavy price to pay for having adopted more socially-just locations in the first place. At present it would seem possible that more retail chains will be prepared to take out-of-town hypermarket proposals to appeal, in the expectation of a permission from the Secretary of State, rather than try to develop on cramped inner-city sites. If such a policy is seen to succeed, planners at local or county level may find that no one is prepared to accept the risks of developing on sites that are socially preferable. Note, however, that there are precedents, as in York, where a superstore had to be located non-centrally and it will be seen later how this can be made socially acceptable.

A WAY FORWARD
A first consideration for planners should, then, be to estimate the penalties imposed upon a retailer when a certain type of site is insisted upon. Town and District centres may not all be, as Schiller (1979, p.11) put it:

"considered unsatisfactory by retailer, planner and shopper alike."

Nevertheless, some town and district centres are, at present, not at all suitable for the type of large scale grocery store that the retailers want to develop and that the shopper, particularly the less advantaged shopper, wishes to be able to use. It is proposed here that two types of solution may be seen as feasible. The first, and preferable solution is to make a realistic assessment of the capacity of town or district centres to accommodate a large store and to move away from 'negative' planning. The experience of ASDA has been that this is far more straightforward where a new centre is proposed and where the shopping facilities may be purpose-built and designed with the housing. The established district centres, on the other hand, are fraught with problems and Havant Borough Council officers may be commended for earmarking a site that was eventually to accommodate an ASDA superstore of proven popularity. However, there were difficulties associated with this site that stemmed from the fact that the land was in multiple ownership. Developers of town and district centre sites are familiar with the delays that follow from multiple ownership. In some sites it has been the experience that small landowners may charge exorbitant amounts for their land, aware that development cannot proceed without them.

Parking is another substantial problem for a superstore needs at least one parking space for every 100 square feet of gross floor space. This would imply 600 car parking spaces allocated exclusively for patrons of ASDA, Waterlooville. If other shoppers are permitted to use the car park then the allowances should rise accordingly. It is axiomatic that these should be 'at grade' car parking spaces to facilitate the use of heavily-laden shopping trolleys. All retailers are aware that costs rise astronomically if car parking spaces have to be provided in multi-storey car parks, underground, or on the store roof.

The circulatory system of the local roads also bears consideration. The ASDA store at Waterlooville opened before the new road layout and a pedestrianisation scheme had been completed. For a period of nine months traffic congestion in Waterlooville was extreme. ASDA were eventually forced to post leaflets to homes in the catchment area pointing out that the roads were completed, congestion ended, and the store was once more accessible. The Waterlooville site is, as one might imagine, not ideal for servicing by heavy and long vehicles, but it is by no means as unsatisfactory as some city centres in this respect.

It is clear that a series of penalties accrued to ASDA Waterlooville that were avoided by Havant Hypermarket. Sparks (1983) has similarly considered the relative locational costs of the inner city – a more extreme instance than that outlined here. Nevertheless, there has been considerable attention paid to retailing in central locations, mostly as political interest in such locations has become heightened. Two of the more valuable contributions have been by NEDO (1981) and especially URPI (1977) where the latter outlined, at a time when the Community Land Act was still extant, a whole range of initiatives for inner areas in general and district centres in particular. Even at that stage, the prospect was that many district centres would not be able to accommodate superstores. Jones (URPI, 1977) drew a useful contrast between 'inner' and 'suburban' district centres and it is notable that ASDA Waterlooville located in the latter. One possible initiative, discussed by Duerden (URPI, 1977) and later by Hallsworth (1984b) was the introduction of community facilities into such centres. This would add another attraction or 'magnet' to complement a superstore and add further to the list of reasons for wishing to visit a particular district centre.

Nevertheless, it remains the case that on many grounds - catchment area, parking, economic situation, even 'image' - some district centres are never going to attract either retailers or consumers. There is a distinct order of preference for centres, beginning with new, suburban, district centres anchoring a modern private housing development in Southern England at the apex. Declining, inner-city district centres in derelict development areas elsewhere in the country form the base. It is not easy to imagine how the latter are going to attract modern, large scale, low priced grocery shopping for their disadvantaged residents. As was noted initially, planners presently have only negative powers. They cannot force retailers into locations that are not in some way attractive to them, but they can 'earmark' sites that are the best compromise available to them.

IMPLICATIONS FOR DISTRICT CENTRE TRADERS

The thrust of the present research has been to consider the welfare implications of superstores from the perspective of the consumer. It is useful, however, to spend a little time considering the welfare implications for the centres that come to receive superstores. Some have suggested that a hypermarket 'creaming off trade all round' is likely to have less impact on trade in one specific centre whereas a superstore might concentrate its effects on the host centre. Quite simply, the most drastic effect would be on foodstores in the centre in general and upon High Street supermarkets in particular as the trade diversion figures given by Hallsworth (1981b, p.26) reveal. At the same time, it has to be recognised that many of the High Street multiples that are being affected by superstores in their locality are themselves developing superstores that are having just the same effects on other traders elsewhere. In simple terms the large-scale grocery goods market is undergoing comprehensive change which occasionally has deleterious effects upon the trade of particular outlets of retail grocery chains. One should also recognise that the retail system is never in equilibrium because change, not stability, is a fact of life in retailing.

Whilst superstore impact is felt locally, so too are the benefits of possible increased traffic by foot for those retailers alert enough to exploit the fact. It may be that the retailer will need to alter the range of goods sold or make other adjustments, but potential usually follows the opening of a superstore. Although it has been stated that effects on other traders are not paramount in this discussion, the purpose is to offer advice on store locations and the side-effects for retailers as well as shoppers must be noted. Locally, attention has been paid to the effects of in-centre superstores; Hallsworth (1979a, 1982a, 1982b, 1984a, 1984b, 1985f) Although actual trading data could not be obtained, all the secondary measures used suggested that superstore competition fell well behind parking and other factors affecting trading when competitors were asked to assess future prospects. The more general point that trading conditions constantly change, was emphasised by Hallsworth (1985f, p.10):

"As has previously been argued (Hallsworth, 1984), superstores, when carefully sited, should be useful agents of positive change. Centres are, however, constantly changing as comparison with a mapping of Waterlooville in, say, 1959, would instantly reveal. The substantial post-war growth in real disposable income in general and the development of supermarkets in particular, will have wrought more changes on the High Street grocery scene in the last forty years than the current trend to superstores. Considering stability rather than change it can be noted that, for the period 1979-1984, 89 Waterlooville units showed no change at all. Another fourteen retained the same function having changed name but often not having changed ownership. Change, *per se*, is a fact of trading life. This paper has shown that its causes may be complex and its effects not always detrimental."

Ridgway (1976, 1981) too, as one might expect, was at pains to point out that superstores bring change but also growth. A centre with a superstore is more attractive overall than a centre without a superstore. In some ways, the arguments of Ridgway parallel those of Guy (1980, p.148), where preferred superstore locations are expressed in a trade-off matrix. Superstores are examined with respect to the following types of factors: containment and amenity; traffic; availability of suitable sites; economic impact; accessibility. These can be seen as the areas that have concerned planners in their consideration of advantageous and disadvantageous locations.

With reference to established district centres, as is the concern here, the advantages would be seen as a maximising of accessibility by all forms of transport.

In Guy's (1980) formulation, however, impact on local trade was seen as exclusively negative. It is felt here that this need not always be so since there can be an 'upgrading' effect from the presence of the attractive new superstore. Evidence that centres can be 'pulled up' by new shopping floorspace is provided by the work of Agergard, Olsen and Allpass (1970). In this, the authors expound their 'theory of spiral movement'. They express change in terms of internal factors (to a centre), these being price, service, assortment (range), outcome and external factors - primarily change in income in the surrounding area. Their analysis, it must be admitted, is couched in terms of competition "for a share of the increased and changed consumption pattern". (1970, p.56). Less attention is paid to decline, although Hallsworth (1976) notes that the work of Golledge (1971) was valuable in this respect. However, Agergard *et al* (1970) see "development of the external factors" as causing "an increase in the size and degree of specialism of the shops" a finding reflecting the work of Berry (1966) and many subsequent authors. The important point is the emphasis on a continuous process of interaction.

As new store types develop, other stores in the same field modify and change. Kirby (1976) expresses similar finding with specific regard to food retailing. A vital point made by Agergard *et al* (1970, p.65-66) is:

"Large shop units which have grown greatly in
importance (supermarkets) ... find their customers
in a geographically more extensive, but not so
intensively-utilised trading area than the small
shop would have done. When a large unit is
located in an existing retail concentration it
means that this centre will not only attract a
greater proportion of the available consumption
in its existing trading area but expand its
influence to the trading areas of adjacent
centres."

The implication is clear: placing a superstore in a district centre should raise the 'status' for the centre, presumably to the benefit of all traders in the centre. Note, however, that the theory also suggests that this will lead to a rise in the range and quality of stores in the centre. Rival retailers will have to adapt to the new store and to the raised and changed patterns arising from it. The addition of a new superstore is therefore both a benefit to the centre as a whole, but also a challenge to existing traders to change in order to profit. This study subscribes to the efficacy of this viewpoint.

MAXIMISING BENEFIT FROM FUTURE LOCATIONS
It must be clear that not all district centres can be made acceptable and it would be pious to believe that steps should be taken to keep superstores only in such centres. All but the very few where development sites are already in evidence seem ill-equipped to attract, or keep, large modern new superstores yet there is still hope that consumers from such areas can shop at superstores. At root, the key objective is to facilitate access to modern, large-scale grocery shopping with cheap prices for those (the disadvantaged) who need those cheap prices, rather than for those best able (the advantaged) to reach any store wherever its location. The retailers need a mix of consumers that must include those who spend heavily on their shopping trips. If the advantaged cannot be persuaded to visit superstores in run-down, inaccessible, unattractive district centres, can the disadvantaged find a way to reach superstores placed where the advantaged will use them?

An answer to this type of question is already being provided by some sectors of the superstore trade. ASDA have a long history of providing buses to reach their superstores - an early example was the ASDA store at Huntington, near York, where the city could not accommodate a superstore. Tesco, however, provide the best evidence for the possibilities of bussing. Tesco, too, sponsored the report by Davies and Champion (1980) which envisaged three possible types of development located to aid the disadvantaged inner-city shopper. These were: superstores in District Centres; superstores in large traditional shopping centres; superstores freestanding in the inner city. Since that time, in the light of trading experience, Tesco PLC has become more inclined to seek freestanding off-centre sites where greater profits can be generated. However, this has been allied to a comprehensive scheme to 'bus-in' shoppers - usually from local authority estates. This may be a function of Tesco's own traditional market segmentation, but the advisability of such a scheme is echoed in this area by Havant Hypermarket itself. Some two years after opening, the store initiated a free bus service from Hayling Island, Bosham, Portchester and Paulsgrove, Wecock Farm and Widley, and Petersfield on selected days of the week. The purpose was to collect shoppers from the major population clusters in the shopping area. The boost to the number of shoppers at the store has made the venture worthwhile and shoppers can remain at the store for approximately two hours before catching a free bus home.

A sensible way forward would be for authorities with district centres that cannot accommodate superstores but which are continuing to receive superstore applications, to insist that the poor are not left behind. The best way to minimise that risk would be to nominate acceptable sites - much in the manner suggested by Gransby (1985). These should be sites acceptable to superstore operators but still located as near as possible to the local 'disadvantaged' groups. Those disadvantaged groups, clearly identified by the planners on welfare criteria related to mobility, should be served by a free bus provided by the store developers and a compromise might thereby be achieved. Those District authorities with new or 'superstore-viable' district centres should work to make these as acceptable as possible to the retailers. Sites should be accumulated where possible, road schemes should be designed with the capacity to handle superstore traffic. Above all, as Hallsworth (1984a) has demonstrated, parking that is free and at ground level should be in plentiful supply. If these criteria cannot be met then the district centre must be deemed unsuitable for superstores and a fringe site with good bus provision should be provided.

It must, however, be emphasised that location in a district centre, where possible, is to be preferred on all grounds. These centres are usually already very accessible so there is no duplication of bus provision or increase in energy costs. Furthermore, it has been demonstrated that the lower income groups in particular tend to use the shopping trip as an opportunity to undertake visits to other shops and services. Indeed, it is necessary to strive to continue to improve access and accessibility to district centres that have already attracted superstores. Now that national attitudes on store location are liberalising, it would be an unfair penalty upon superstores that have already chosen a more socially just location to find their trading area eroded by a new store with better accessibility to the high-spending higher income groups. Were that to happen, and there is evidence that some existing stores are being undercut by new rivals, it would only be natural to expect all store chains to seek the 'economically optimal' site in future. That said, in the event of a future oil crisis, the nature of the 'optimal' location would swing back in favour of the more centrally-located store. The compromise suggested above should allow stores to remain viable under a wide range of general economic conditions.

It may seem that the proposals noted above are essentially unadventurous. The aim is not to produce 'ideal' outcomes that are wildly unrealistic and unlikely to come to fruition, but moderate, practical, pragmatic and workable ideas. One cannot begin to estimate what trading conditions will be like in a few years' time. Attempts to be dogmatic about future outcomes simply lead to the type of inadequate, inflexible plan that has bedevilled British town and country planning for forty years. The system of land ownership – that brings windfall profits for the fortunate few who own land that comes to be developed for a superstore – is not going to change in the foreseeable future. Site difficulties and operating costs will remain a key factor working against district centres and this is why many will never be suitable for superstores. On the other hand, there need be no reason why local authority owned land should not be made available for food superstores at a reasonable price. This would forestall the 'windfall profits' to the private landowner and also reduce overheads for the food retailer. Some areas, of course, simply will not have the purchasing power ever to support a superstore.

Indeed, for some groups in society, the key retail issues will not be locational ones at all. For certain family types with a need to shop around a work schedule, the really meaning-ful developments will concern liberalising of shop opening hours or Sunday trading. Both are issues beyond the scope of this study. Where locational criteria are of key concern it is to be hoped that planners will be more flexible, positive and pragmatic in future and will, hopefully, bring about the best possible outcomes in welfare terms.

At root, these suggestions call for a revision of the present structure of the retail system that is shown in Figure 7.1. The diagram depicts the planners and the retailers as operating from opposing ends of a spectrum, with national influence s overarching both. It is increasingly the nature of the British political system that control by central Government is the ultimate influence on outcomes, so little change may be anticipated there. What can happen is a formalisation of the informal type of process undertaken by ASDA when considering a site in Havant Borough. Their preparedness to seek planner co-operation allowed them to be led away from their initial choice of site into a successful district centre location proposed by the planners. Delay only ensued because of a subsequent decision by the local authority to prepare a develop-ment brief. Figure 7.2 suggests that such meetings should be part of an interactive process and that planners should actively seek sites within their area that retailers might adopt. This requires the planners to acquire the ability to judge what is

162

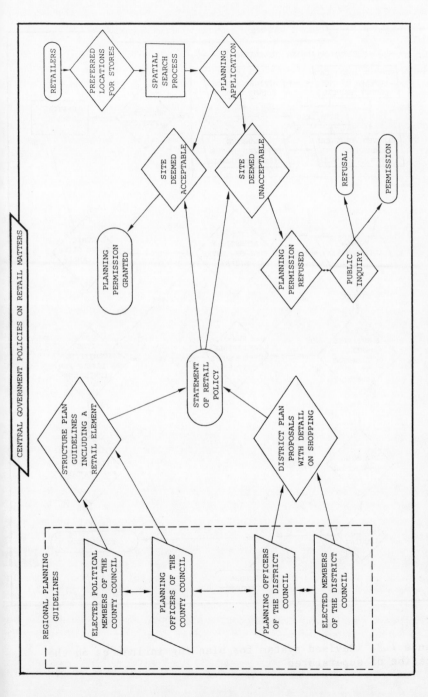

Figure 7.1   Planning influences on the location of superstores

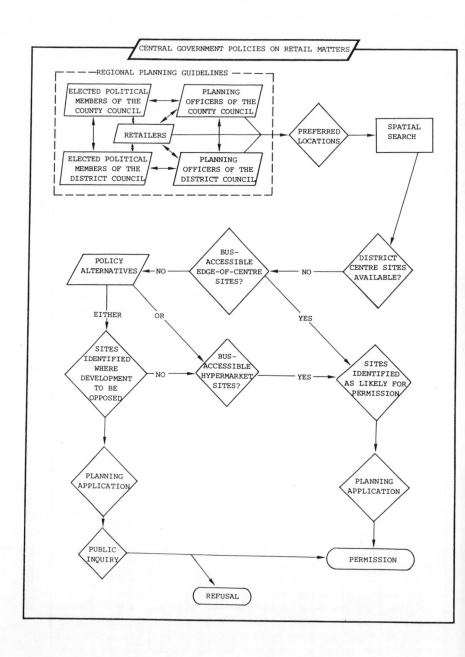

Figure 7.2   Revised system for planning influences on the
location of superstores

and what is not a viable superstore site. They must also be prepared to concede that their area may have no possibilities for superstore development.

Above all, there will be the requirement for a real effort of political will. Local politicians (and this issue has become increasingly a District, not County, matter) must face up to the reality that traders and customers alike demand superstores. There is evidence that politicians have refused planning permission for stores despite being fully aware that the store in question would obviously succeed on appeal to the Minister. They have not been prepared to accept direct responsibilty for fear of criticism in some local quarters – but their actions have imposed costs upon developers that must eventually be borne by consumers. Indeed, present legislation may force the costs of such refusals back on the Councils themselves. Figure 7.2, then, is perhaps less modest than it appears in terms of the changed attitudes that will be required in order to bring its concepts to fruition. The diagram represents a search process and some planners will find that their district centre cannot possibly accommodate a superstore. They will then have to search for the next best alternative that gives a viable site and accessibility for the poorer sectors of society. Furthermore, they will have to indicate that this is an acceptable site for which planning permission will be forthcoming. If this is in local authority ownership, so much the better; with planning permission on offer, good bus links can be insisted upon. The alternative, of total opposition to all forms of decentralised food retailing, will benefit no-one and solutions will be imposed by the planning appeal system and the chance to insist upon bus provision may be lost. That would be a tragedy for all parties concerned, with negative welfare implications that can, with forethought and a recognition of political reality, easily be avoided.

These proposals, relating only to food shopping, present a way forward from what is currently seen as deadlock. Attitudes at the Department of the Environment seem certain to move further in the direction of liberalising market processes. This creates conflict with County and Local Planners, with those concerned for the welfare of the less mobile and, to an extent, with the retailers themselves. The retailers have become used to a system of 'modifiable restraint'. They have become used to knowing where a permission will be forthcoming immediately and where the plan might go to appeal. They have decades of experience in adjusting to modest restraint. If the controls were totally abandoned there would be very considerable unease particularly from those in locations like ASDA Waterlooville which might be undercut by rivals nearer to the high-spending sectors of the population. Present attitudes at the Department of the Environment suggest a 'free market' emphasis - but Britain does not have a 'free' retail market. Such is the power of multiple chains that the system is at least partly oligopolistic. The retailers truly do not want a free market 'free for all'. It seems highly likely that many would in fact welcome the positive steps here outlined as a sensible way forward.

Bibliography

ABURN A A (1973) "Shopping patterns in an urban area", Proc. Seventh New Zealand Conf, 57-64. New Zealand Geographical Society, Hamilton, New Zealand.

ADAMS J S (1969) "Directional bias in intra-urban migration", Economic Geography, 45, 302-23.

ADAMS-WEBBER J (1970a) "An analysis of the discriminant validity of several repertory grid indices", British Journal of Pyschology, 61, 83-90.

ADAMS-WEBBER J (1970b) "Elicited versus provided constructs in repertory grid technique; a review", British Journal of Medical Psychology, 43, 349-354.

ADCOCK C J (1954) Factorial Analysis for Non-Mathematicians, Melbourne UP.

AGERGARD E, OLSEN P A, and ALLPASS J (1970) "The interaction between retailing and the urban centre structure: a theory of spiral movement", Environment and Planning, 2, 55-71.

ALEXANDER I and DAWSON J A (1979) "Employment in retailing, a case study of employment in suburban shopping centres", Geoforum, 10, 407-25.

ALEXANDER I and DAWSON J A (1979) "Suburbanization of retailing sales and employment in Australian cities", Australian Geographical Studies, 76-83.

AMBROSE P J (1967) "An analysis of intra-urban shopping patterns", Town Planning Review, 38, 327-34.

ANDERSON T W (1958), Introduction to Multivariate Statistical Analysis, New York, John Wiley and Sons, Inc.

ANDREASEN A R (1965) "Attitudes and customer behaviour: a decision model" in Preston L (Ed) New Research in Marketing, Institute of Business and Economic Research, University of California, Berkeley.

ANDREWS H F (1971) "Consumer behaviour and the tertiary activity system" in Wilson A G (Ed), Urban and Regional Planning, Pion, London.

APPLEBAUM W (1965) "Measuring retail market penetration for a discount food super-market: a case study", Journal of Retailing, 41, 1-15.

BANNISTER D (1962b) "Personal construct theory: a summer and experimental paradigm", Acta Psychologica, 20, 104-120.

BANNISTER D and MAIR J M M (1968) The Evaluation of Personal Constructs, Academic Press, London.

BATTY M (1978) "Urban Models in the planning process", in Herbert D T and Johnston R J (Eds) Geography and the Urban Environment, Vol 1, Wiley, London, 63-134.

BEAUJEU-GARNIER J and DELOBEZ A (1977) La Geographie du Commerce, Masson, Paris.

BELL T (1973) "A discussion of the relevance of Kelly's theory to architectural theory", Kingston Polytechnic Architectural Psychology Working Paper No. 1.

BENDER M P (1974) "Provided versus elicited constructs: an explanation of Warr & Coffman's (1970) anomalous finding", British Journal of Social and Clinical Psychology, 13, 329.

BENNISON D J & DAVIES R L (1977), "The movement of shoppers within the central area of Newcastle Upon Tyne", University of Newcastle upon Tyne, Department of Geography, Seminar Papers, 34.

BERMAN L (1982) "Statistics of the distributive trades", paper presented to Statistics users Conference on the Distributive Trades, Royal Society, London.

BERMOND R (1976) The Disadvantages of Inequality, McDonald & Jones (PEP), London.

BERNSTEIN B (1958) "Some sociological determinants of perception", British Journal of Sociology, 9, 159-74.

BERNSTEIN B (1961) "Social class and linguistic development", pp288-314 in Economy, Education and Society, Eds Halsey, Floud, & Anderson, New York.

BERRY B J L, BARNUM H G & TENNANT R J (1962) "Retail location and consumer behaviour," Papers and Proceedings of the Regional Science Association, 9, 65-106.

BERRY B J L (1963) "Commercial structure and commercial blight", University of Chicago, Department of Geography, Research Paper, 85.

168

BERRY B J L (1967b) Geography of Market Centres and Retail Distribution, Prentice-Hall, Englewood Cliffs, New Jersey.

BOAL F W & JOHNSON D B (1965) "The functions of retail and service establishments on commercial ribbons", Canadian Geographer, 9, 145-69.

BOWLBY S R (1979) "Accessibility, mobility and shopping provision", in Goodall B and Kirby A (Eds), Resources & Planning, Oxford, 293-323.

BOWLBY S (1981) "Planning for women to shop", Draft mimeo, University of Reading.

BRIDGES M (1976) The York Asda, A Study of Changing Shopping Patterns Around a Superstore, University of Manchester, Centre for Urban and Regional Planning.

BROOKER-GROSS S R (1981) "Shopping behavior in two sets of shopping destinations: an interactionalist interpretation of outshopping", Tijdschrift voor Economische en Sociale Geografie, 72, 28-34.

BROOM D and GUY C M (1983) "Accessibility and mobility as determinants of shopping behaviour" paper presented to meeting of the Quantitative methods Study Group of the Institute of British Geographers, September 1983, Sheffield.

BRUMMELL A C and E J HARRISON (1974) Behavioural Geography and Multi-dimensional Scaling, Discussion paper 1, Department of Geography, McMaster University, Canada.

BRUCE A (1974) "Why we shop where we do", Built Environment, 3, 280-4.

BRUCE A J and DELWORTH K (1976) "Shopping behaviour in four areas", Building Res. Estab. Note N3/76, Garston, Herts.

BRUCE G D (1969) "The ecological structure of retail institutions" Journal of Marketing Research, 5(1), 48-53.

BUCKLIN L P (1967a) "Competitive impact of a new supermarket", Journal of Marketing Research, 4, 356-61.

BUCKLIN L P (1971) "Retail gravity models and consumer choice : A theoretical and empirical critique", Economic Geography, 47, 489-97.

BUNGE W (1962) Theoretical Geography, Lund Studies in Geography, Series C No. 1 Gleerup, Lund.

BUNTING T E and GUELKE L (1979) "Behavioral and perception geography : a critical appraisal", Annals of the Association of American Geographers, 69, 448-62.

BURNS W (1959) British Shopping Centres, Leonard Hill, London.

BURGESS R G (1982) Field Research : A Source Book and Field Manual, London, Allen & Unwin.

BURT S et al (1983) "Structure plans and retailing policies", The Planner, 69(1), 11-13.

BUURSINK J (1981) "On testing the nearest centre hypotheis", Tijdschrift voor Economische en Sociale Geografie, 72(1), 47-49.

CADWALLADER M (1975) "A behavioural model of consumer spatial decisionmaking", Economic Geography, 51, 339-49.

CADWALLADER M (1981) "Towards a cognitive gravity model : the case of consumer spatial behaviour", Regional Studies, 15(4), 275-84.

CANNELL C and KAHN R (1966) "The collection of data by interviewing", Chap 8 in Festinger L and Katz D (1966) Research Methods in the Behavioural Sciences, Holt-Rinehart-Winston, New York.

CANTER D and THORNE R (1972) "Attitudes to housing", Environment & Behaviour, 4(1), 3-31.

CAPLOVITZ D (1967) The Poor Pay More, The Free Press, New York.

CARTER H and ROWLEY G (1966) "The morphology of the central business district of Cardiff", Transactions of the Institute of British Geographers, 38, 119-34.

CARTER H (1972) The Study of Urban Geography, Arnold, London.

CASTELLS M (1975) "Immigrant workers and class struggle in advanced capitalism : the Western European experience", Politics and Society, 5, 33-66.

CASTELLS M (1977) The Urban Question, Edward Arnold, London.

CASTELLS M (1978) City, Class and Power, Macmillan, London.

CASTELLS M (1983) "Crisis, planning, and the quality of life : managing the new historical relationships between space and society", Environment and Planning D : Society and Space, 1, 3-21.

CATTELL A S and TILLY C (1960) "The interaction of social and physical space", American Sociological Review, 25, 877-884.

CENTRAL STATISTICAL OFFICE (1984) "Social Trends", London.

CHILDS D and HEDGES R (1980) "The analysis of interpersonal perceptions as a repertory grid", British Journal of Medical Psychology, 53, 127-136.

CHRISTALLER W (1933) Central Places in Southern Germany, Gustav Fischer, Jena.

CLARK W A V (1967), "The spatial structure of retail functions in a New Zealand city", New Zealand Geographer, 23, 23-33.

CLARK W A V (1968) "Consumer travel patterns and the concept of range" Annals of the Association of American Geographers, 58, 386-96.

CLARK W A V and Rushton G (1970) "Models of intra-urban consumer behaviour and their implications for central place theory", Economic Geography, 46, 486-97.

COATES B E, JOHNSTON R J and KNOX P L (1977) Geography and Inequality, Oxford.

COELHO J D and WILSON A G (1976) "The optimum location and size of shopping centres", Regional Studies, 10, 413-21.

COLE H R (1966) "Shopping assessments at Haydock and elsewhere: a review", Urban Studies, 3, 147-56.

CONVERSE P D (1949) "New laws of retail gravitation", Journal of Marketing.

COSHALL J (1985) "The form of micro-spatial consumer cognition and its congruence with search behaviour", Tijdschrift voor Economische en Sociale Geografie, 76(5), 345-355.

CRAIK K (1968) "The comprehension of the everyday physical environment", Journal American Institute of Planners, 34, 29-37.

CULLEN J D (1980) "Image, ideology and urban mangerialism" unpubl. Ph.D thesis, Univ of Dundee.

CULLEN J D and KNOX P L (1981) "The triumph of the eunuch: planners, urban managers and the suppression of political opposition", Urban Aff. Quart, 17(2), 149-72.

CULLINGWORTH J D (1972) Town and Country Planning in Britain, Allen & Unwin, London.

DANIELS P W and WARNES A M (1980) Movement in Cities : Spatial Perspectives on Urban Transport and Travel, Methuen, London.

DAULTREY S (1976) Principal Components Analysis, Catmog 8, Geobooks, Norwich.

DAVIES K & SPARKS L (1981), "Policies for the location of large stores", Area, 13, 232-5.

DAVIES R L (1968) "Effects of consumer income differences on the business provisions of small shopping centres", Urban Studies, 5, 144-64.

DAVIES R L (1969) "Effects of consumer income differences on shopping movement behavior", Tijdschrift voor Economische en Sociale Geografie, 60, 111-21.

DAVIES R L (1970) "Issues in retailing", in R L Davies and P Hall (Eds), Issues in Urban Society, Penguin.

DAVIES R L (1972a), "The retail pattern of the central area of Coventry", Institute of British Geographers, Urban Study Group, Occasional Publication, 1, 1-32.

DAVIES R L (1972b) "Structural models of retail distribution", Transactions of the Institute of British Geographers 57, 59-82

DAVIES R L (1973a) "The location of service activities" in Chisholm M and Rodgers B (Eds), Studies in Human Geography, Heinemann, London.

DAVIES R L (1973b) "Evaluation of retail store attributes and sales performance", European Journal of Marketing, 7, 89-102.

DAVIES R L (1973c) "Patterns and profiles of consumer behaviour", Research Series No 10, Department of Geography, University of Newcastle-upon-Tyne, Northumberland.

DAVIES R L (1976) Marketing Geography - with Special Reference to Retailing, Retailing and Planning Associates, Corbridge, Northumberland, and (1977) Methuen, London.

DAVIES R L (1977b), "A framework for commercial planning policies", Town Planning Review, 49, 42-58.

DAVIES R L (1977c) "Issues in retailing", Chapter 5 in
Davies R L and Hall P (Eds) Issues in Urban Society, Penguin,
Harmondsworth.

DAVIES R L (1979), Retail Planning in the European Community,
Saxon House.

DAVIES R L (1984) Retail and Commercial Planning, Croom Helm,
London.

DAVIES R L and BENNISON D J (1978) "Retailing in the city
centre: the characters of shopping streets", Tijdschrift
voor Economische en Sociale Geografie, 69, 270-85.

DAVIES R L and CHAMPION A G (1980a) "Social inequities in
shopping opportunities: how the private sector can respond",
Tesco Stores Holdings Ltd, Cheshunt, Herts.

DAVIES R L and KIRBY D (1980b) "Retail Organisation" Chapter 3
in Dawson J A, Retail Geography, Croom Helm, London.

DAVIES W K D (1966) "The ranking of service centres : a
critical review", Transactions of the Institute of British
Geographers, 40, 51-65.

DAVIES W K D (1968) "The morphology of central places: a case
study", Annals of the Association of American Geographers,
58, 91-110.

DAVIES W K D (1971) "Varimax and the destruction of Generality",
Area, 3(2), 112-118.

DAWS L F and BRUCE A J (1971) Shopping in Watford, Building
Research Establishment, Watford.

DAWS L F and McCULLOCH M (1974) "On shoppers' requirements for
the location of shops in towns (Building Research Establishment, Current Paper, 23).

DAWSON J A (1973) "Marketing geography" in Dawson J A and
Doornkamp J C (Eds) Evaluating the Human Environment : Essays
in Applied Geography.

DAWSON J A (1974) "The suburbanisation of retail activity" in
J H Johnson (Ed) Suburban Growth, Wiley, London.

DAWSON J A (1976a) "Hypermarkets in France", Geography, 61,
259-62.

DAWSON J A and KIRBY D A (1976) "Woolco at Cwmbran: how
retailers view it", Retail and Distribution Management, 4.

DAWSON J A (1979a), The Marketing Environment, London,
Croom Helm.

DAWSON J A (1979b), "Retail trends in the EEC", in Davies R L
(Ed), Retail Planning in the European Community, Saxon House,
21-49.

DAWSON J A (1980a) (Ed) Retail Geography, Croom Helm, London.

DAWSON J A (1980b) Research priorities in retail geography,
Interim report of SSRC-sponsored seminar group on geography
of retailing.

DAWSON J A and KIRBY D A (1980) (Eds) Geography and the Urban
Environment : Progress in Research and Applications, Volume
III, John Wiley, London.

DAWSON J A (1981) "Shopping centres in France" Geography, 66, 143-6.

DAWSON J A (1983) "Retail Impact Studies", The Planner, 69(1), 25.

DAY R A (1973) "Consumer shopping behaviour in a planned urban environment", Tijdschrift voor Economische en Sociale Geografie, 64, 77-85.

DEAR M and CLARK G (1981) "The state in capitalism and the capitalist state", in Dear M and Scott A (Eds) Urbanisation and Urban Planning in Capitalist Society.

DEPARTMENT OF EMPLOYMENT (1985) Department of Employment Gazette.

DEPARTMENT OF THE ENVIRONMENT (1972) Development Control Policy Note 13: Out of Town Shops and Shopping Centres, HMSO, London.

DEPARTMENT OF THE ENVIRONMENT (1972, 1978) Decision Letters, Eastleigh Carrefour, Bedhampton PIMCO.

DEPARTMENT OF THE ENVIRONMENT (1976a) "The Eastleigh Carrefour: a hypermarket and its effects", DoE Research Report 16, HMSO, London.

DEPARTMENT OF THE ENVIRONMENT (1976b) Large New Stores, DoE Circular 71/76 HMSO, London.

DEPARTMENT OF THE ENVIRONMENT (1977) Development Control Policy Note 13 : Large New Stores, HMSO, London.

DEPARTMENT OF THE ENVIRONMENT (1985) The Use of Conditions in Planning Permissions, Circular 1/85, HMSO.

DEPARTMENTS OF THE ENVIRONMENT & TRANSPORT (1978) "The Eastleigh Carrefour hypermarket after three years", DoE and T Research Report 27, HMSO, London.

DONALDSONS (1976) "Planning inquiry study", Donaldsons Research Report 3, London.

DONALDSONS (1978) "Planning inquiry study two", Donaldsons Research Report 5, London.

DOWNS R M (1970) "The cognitive structure of an urban shopping centre", Environment and Behaviour, 2, 13-39.

DOWNS R M (1979) "Critical appraisal or determined philosphical scepticism", Annals of the Association of American Geographers, 69, 468-71.

DOWNS R M and STEA D (Eds) (1973) Image and Environment, Aldine, Chicago.

DOWNS R M and STEA D (1977) Maps in Minds, Harper and Row, New York.

DREWETT R, GODDARD J, and SPENCER N (1974) "Urban Change in Britain: 1966-1971", Working Paper No. 1 Department of Geography, LSE London.

DREWETT R GODDARD J and SPENCE N (1976) "British Cities urban population and employment trends", DoE Research Report 10, London.

DUNCAN O D and DUNCAN B (1955) "Residential distribution and occupational stratification", American Journal of Sociology, 60, 493-503.

DUNN R and WRIGLEY N (1984) "Store loyalty for grocery products : an empirical study", Area, 16, 307-14.

EBDON D (1977) Statistics in Geography, Blackwells, London.

ELIOT-HURST M E (1969) "The structure of movement and household travel behaviour", Urban Studies, 6, 1-17.

ESTATES GAZETTE (1973) Hypermarkets in perspective, 228, Nov 3, 825.

ESTATES GAZETTE (1973) Hypermarkets, 234, 133 & 341.

EUROMONITOR (1983) "Hypermarkets and Superstores", Euromonitor publications 1983, London.

EVANS A & RICHARDSON R (1979) "Patterns of urban unemployment", Discussion Paper No 2, Dept of Economics, University of Reading.

EYLES J D (1971) "Putting new sentiments into old theories : how else can we look at behavioural patterns?", Area, 3, 242-250.

EYLES J D and LEE R (1982) "Human Geography in Explanation", Transactions of the Institute of British Geographers, 7, 1, 117-122.

FERNIE J and CARRICK R J (1981) "Quasi-retail activity in Britain", paper presented at the annual conference of the Institute of British Geographers, Leicester.

FIELD F (1979) The Wealth Report, RKP, London.

FINANCIAL TIMES (1986) "Retail Store Chains", July 19.

FINGLETON B (1975) "A factorial approach to the nearest centre hypothesis", Transactions of the Institute of British Geographers, 65, 131-39.

FINNEY J (1976) In "Hypermarkets and superstores" URPI, UI.

FINNEY J E and ROBINSON J (1976) "District shopping centres : some case studies" Proceedings of the Seminar on Retailing, PTRC Summer Annual Meeting.

FOTHERINGHAM A S (1986) "Market share analysis techniques, a review and illustration of current US practise", paper presented to ESRC workshop Bristol, February.

FOXALL G R (1977) Consumer behaviour: a practical guide, Retailing and Planning Associates, Corbridge, Nothumberland.

FRANSELLA F (1976) "The theory and measurement of personal constructs", in Granville-Grossman (Ed), Recent Advances in Clinical Psychiatry, Churchill Livingstone, London.

FRANSELLA F and ADAMS B (1966) "An illustration of the use of repertory grid technique in a clinical setting", British Journal of Social and Clinical Psychology, 5, 51-62.

FRANSELLA F and BANNISTER P (1977) A Manual for Repertory Grid Technique, Academic Press, London.

FROST W A K (1969) "The development of a technique for TV programme assessment", Journal of the Market Research Society, 11, 25-44.

FRUCHTER B (1954) Introduction to Factor Analysis, New York, Van Nostrand.

GANTVOORT J T (1971) "Shopping centre versus town centre",
Town Planning Review, 42, 61-70.
GARNER B J (1966) "The internal structure of retail nuclea-
tions", North Western Studies in Geography, 12.
GAYLER H J (1980) "Social class and consumer spatial behaviour
: some aspects of variation in shopping patterns in metro-
politan Vancouver, Canada", Transactions of the Institute of
British Geographers, NS, 5, 427-45.
GINSBERG M (1965) On Justice in Society, Penguin, Harmondsworth.
GOLDMAN A (1975), "The use of landmarks in recalling retail
stores," Urban Studies, 12, 319-24.
GOLLEDGE R G and BROWN L A (1967) "Search, learning, and the
market decision process", Geografiska Annaler, 49B.
GOODCHILD B (1974) "Class differences in environmental
perception: an exploratory study", Urban Studies, 11, 157-69.
GOLLEDGE R G, RUSHTON G and CLARK W A V (1966) "Some spatial
characteristics of Iowa's dispersed farm population and
their implications for the grouping of central place
functions", Economic Geography, 42, 261-272.
GOLLEDGE R and ZANNARAS G (1970) "The perception of urban
structure", EDRA 2 Proceedings, 111-121.
GOULD P R (1967) "On the geographical interpretation of
Eigenvalues", Transactions of the Institute of British
Geographers, 42, 53-86.
GRANSBY D (1984) "Cooperation or conflict", Proceedings, PTRC
12th annual summer meeting and exhibition, Brighton, 45-50.
GRAY F (1975) "Non-explanation in urban geography", Area, 7,
228-235.
GUY C M (1976a) "Neighbourhood shops in new towns"' Town and
Country Planning, 44, 221-224.
GUY C M (1976b) "A method of examining and evaluating the
impact of major retail developments upon existing shops and
their users", Environment and Planning, A9, 491-504.
GUY C M (1980) Retail Location and Retail Planning in Britain,
Gower, London.
GUY C M (1983) "Household income and food shopping behaviour",
Unit Retail Plan. Inf. Information Brief 83/5, Reading.
GUY C M (1984a) "Superstore shopping in Cardiff", Unit Retail
Plan. Inf. Information Brief 84/5, Reading.
GUY C M (1984b) "Food and grocery shopping behaviour in the
recession", paper presented to the Annual Conference,
Institute of British Geographers, Durham, January.
GUY C M (1985) "Food and grocery shopping behaviour in Cardiff",
UWIST Papers Plan. Res. No 86.
GUY C M and O'BRIEN L G (1983) "Measurement of grocery prices
: some methodological considerations and empirical results"
J Cons. Stud. Home Econ., 7, 213-27.

GUY C M, WRIGLEY N, O'BRIEN L G and HISCOCKS G (1983) "The Cardiff shopping diary survey : a report on the methodology", UWIST Paps Plann.Res. No 68, Dept of Town Plann. UWIST, Cardiff.

GUY C M, WRIGLEY N and DUNN R (1984) "Some characteristics of Co-operative store use in Cardiff", Co-op. Market. Mgmt, 9, 8-10.

HALL M, KNAPP J and WINSTEN C (1961) Distribution in Great Britain and North America, Oxford University Press, Oxford.

HALL P et al (1973) The Containment of Urban England, George Allen and Unwin, London.

HALL P (1974) Urban and Regional Planning, Penguin, London.

HALL P (1978), "Hypermarkets", New Society, August 10, 1978.

HALLSWORTH A G (1976), "Synthesising central place studies", paper presented to AAG Annual Conference, New York.

HALLSWORTH A G (1978) "A caveat on retail assessment", Area, 10(1), 24-5.

HALLSWORTH A G (1979a) Trading Patterns of an In-Centre Superstore : Tesco, Portsmouth, Portsmouth Polytechnic.

HALLSWORTH A G (1979b) "Structure planning influences on retail development", paper presented to IBG Annual Conference, University of Manchester.

HALLSWORTH A G (1981a) Trading Patterns of a Freestanding Hypermarket : Havant Hypermarket, Portsmouth Polytechnic.

HALLSWORTH A G (1981b) Trading Patterns of a District Centre Superstore : Asda, Waterlooville, Portsmouth Polytechnic.

HALLSWORTH A G (1981c) "An Asda and a Co-op : a comparative study", Retail and Distribution Management, Nov/Dec, 42-45.

HALLSWORTH A G (1981d) "Impact Studies", paper presented to IBG Annual Conference, University of Leicester.

HALLSWORTH A G (1982a) Patterns of Change in Consumer Expenditure in South East Hampshire 1980-1981, Portsmouth Polytechnic.

HALLSWORTH A G (1982b) "Some trader attitudes to superstore development", Retail and Distribution Management, July/Aug, 17-19.

HALLSWORTH A G (1983a) Trading Patterns of a Retail Furnishings Superstore : Brown Bear, Fareham, Portsmouth Polytechnic.

HALLSWORTH A G (1983b) "Fareham's Brown Bear", Retail and Distribution Management, May/June, (with Y K Court).

HALLSWORTH A G (1984a) "Recession and a district centre", paper presented to IBG Annual Conference, Durham.

HALLSWORTH A G (1984b) "Superstores and district centres", paper presented to 12th Annual Summer Meeting and Exhibition, PTRC, University of Sussex, Brighton, July.

HALLSWORTH A G (1985a) "The French furniture market: growth with change", Retail and Distribution Management, 13(2), March/April, 36-38.

HALLSWORTH A G (1985b) "Shopping centres in canada: an emphasis on downtown", Retail and Distribution Management, 13(5), Sept/Oct 22-25.

HALLSWORTH A G (1985c) "British planning policy and large scale foodstores", paper presented to Annual Conference, Association of American Geographers, Detroit, Michigan, USA, April.

HALLSWORTH A G (1985d), "Hypermarkets and superstores", paper presented to Emrys G Bowen Memorial Conference, Aberystwyth, May.

HALLSWORTH A G (1985e) "Consumer perceptions of hypermarkets and superstores", paper presented to 1st International Colloquium, IGU Study Group, Geographie des Activites Commerciales, Sorbonne, Paris, June.

HALLSWORTH A G (1985f) "Retail change in a district centre", paper presented to 13th Annual Summer Meeting & Exhibition, PTRC, Brighton, July.

HAMNETT C (1979) "Area based explanations", in Herbert and Smith Social Problems and the City", Oxford.

HAMPSHIRE COUNTY COUNCIL (1971) Mimeo report.

HAMPSHIRE COUNTY COUNCIL (1972) South Hampshire Structure Plan: Report of Survey, HCC.

HAMPSHIRE COUNTY COUNCIL (1972) South Hampshire Structure Plan: Draft Document for Consultation, HCC.

HAMPSHIRE COUNTY COUNCIL (1977) South Hampshire Structure Plan: Approved Plan with Letter of Modification, HCC.

HAMPSHIRE COUNTY COUNCIL (1978), Shopping Policies in South Hampshire, Draft document.

HANSON S (1977) " Measuring the cognitive levels of urban residents", Geografiska Annaler, 59B, 67-81.

HANSON S (1980), "Spatial diversification and multipurpose travel : implications for choice theory", Geographical Analysis, 12, 245-57.

HARLOE M (Ed) (1974) Captive Cities, Wiley, London.

HARMAN H (1967) Modern Factor Analysis, Second Edition, Chicago, University of Chicago Press.

HARRISON J and SARRE P (1975) "Personal construct theory in the measurement of environmental images", Environment and Behaviour, 7, 3-58.

HARVEY D (1969) Explanation in Geography, Edward Arnold, London.

HARVEY D (1973) Social Justice and the City, Edward Arnold, London.

HARVEY D (1975) "The geography of capitalist accumulation: a reconstruction of the marxian theory", Antipode, 7, 2:9-21.

HARVEY D (1977) "Labour, capital and class struggle around the built environment in advanced capitalist societies", Politics and Society, 6, 265-95.

HARVEY D (1981) "The urban process under capitalism: a frame-
work for analysis", in M Dear and A J Scott (Eds) Urbanization
and Urban Planning in Capitalist Society, Methuen, Andover,
Hants, 91-121.
HAVANT BOROUGH COUNCIL (1977) "Development Brief: South West
Quadrant Waterlooville".
HELMSTADTER G (1970) Research Concepts in Human Behavior, New
York, Appleton Century Crofts.
HERBERT D T and JOHNSTON R J (1978) Geography and the Urban
Environment, Vol 1, John Wiley, London.
HERBERT D T and SMITH D M (Eds) (1979) Social Problems and the
City: Geographical Perspectives, Oxford University Press,
Oxford.
HERBERT D and THOMAS C (1982) Urban Geography, Wiley, Chichester
HILLMAN M et al (1972) Personal Mobility and Transport Policy,
Political and Economic Planning, London, (Policy Studies
Institute).
HILLMAN M (1973) "The social costs of hypermarket developments",
Built Environment, 2, 89-91.
HILLMAN M et al (1976) Transport Realities and Planning Policy,
XLII(567), PEP, London, (Policy Studies Institute).
HOGGART K (1978) "Consumer shopping strategies and purchasing
activity : an exploratory investigation", Geoforum, 9, 415-23.
HOLTERMANN S (1975) "Areas of urban deprivation in Great
Britain : an analysis of 1971 census data", Social Trends,
6, 33-47.
HOTELLING H (1933) "Analysis of a complex of statistical
variables into Principal Components", Journal of Educational
Psychology, 24, 417-41, 498-520.
HUDSON R (1974a) Consumer Spatial Behaviour : A Conceptual
Model and Empirical Investigation, PhD thesis, University of
Bristol.
HUDSON R (1974b) "Images of the retailing environment: an
example of the use of the repertory grid methodology",
Environment and Behavior, 6, 470-94.
HUDSON R (1975) "Patterns of spatial search", Transactions of
the Institute of British Geographers, 65, 141-54.
HUDSON R (1980) "Personal construct theory, the repertory grid
measure and human geography", Progress in Human Geography,
4, 346-59.
HUFF D L (1963) "A probabilistic analysis of shopping centre
trade areas", Land Economics, 39, 81-90.
JENSEN-BUTLER C (1972) "Gravity models as planning tools : a
review of theoretical and operational problems", Geografiska
Annaler, 54B, 68-78.
JOHNSTON R J (1980) City and Society : An Outline for Urban
Geography, Penguin, Harmondsworth.
JONES P M (1978) Trading features of hypermarkets and super-
stores, Unit for Retail Planning Information, Reading.

JONES P (1981) "Retail innovation and diffusion - the spread of Asda stores", Area, 13, 197-201.

KELLY G A (1955) The Psychology of Personal Constructs, Vols 1 and 2, Norton, New York.

KENDALL M (1957) A Course in Multivariate Analysis, Griffin, London.

KERLINGER F N (1964) Foundations of Behavioural Research, New York, Holt, Rinehart and Winston.

KERNER O (1968) Report of the Presidential Commission into Civil Disorders, Washington, USA.

KING L J (1969) Statistical Analysis in Geography, New Jersey, Prentice-Hall, Inc.

KIRBY A M (1981) "Geographic contributions to the inner city debate : a critical assessment", Area, 13(3), 177-181.

KIRBY A M (1983) "On society without space : a critique of Saunder's nonspatial urban sociology", Environment and Planning D: Society and Space 1, 226-233.

KIRBY D A (1974) "Shopkeepers go shopping", Geographical Magazine, 43, 526-528.

KIRBY D A (1975) "The small shop in Britain", Town and Country Planning, 43, 496-500.

KIRBY D A (1976) "The North American convenience store" in: Jones P and Oliphant R (Eds) Local Shops: Problems and Prospects.

KIRBY D A (1978) "Retail assessment", Area, 10(4), 268-70.

KIRBY D A, OLSEN J A, SJOHOLT P and STOLEN J (1981) The Norwegian Aid Programme to Shops in Sparsely Populated Areas, Oslo.

KIRK W (1963) "Problems of geography", Geography, 48, 357-371.

KIVELL P T (1972) "Retailing in non-central locations", in The Retail Structure of Cities, IBG Occasional Publications 1.

KIVELL P T and SHAW G (1980) "The study of retail location", Chapter 2 in Dawson, J (Ed), Retail Geography, Croom Helm, London.

KNOX P L (1975) Social Well-being : a Spatial Perspective, Oxford University Press, Oxford.

KNOX P L (1982b) Urban Social Geography, London.

KNOX P L (1981a) "Town planning and the internal survival mechanisms of urbanized capitalism", Area, 13, 183-8.

KNOX P L and CULLEN J D (1981b) "Planners as urban managers : an exploration of the attitudes and self-image of senior British planners" Environment and Planning, (7), 885-92.

KUUSINEN J and NYSTEDT L (1975b) "Individual versus provided constructs, cognitive complexity and extremity of ratings in person perception", Scandinavian Journal of Psychology, 16, 137-148.

LAING R D (1967) The Politics of Experience, Penguin, Harmondsworth.

LAKSHMANAN T R and HANSEN W G (1965) "A retail market potential model", Journal of the American Institute of Planners, 31, 134-144.

LEE M, JONES P and PEACH C (1973) Caerphilly Hypermarket Study, Donaldsons Research Report, London.

LEE M and KENT E (1975) Caerphilly Hypermarket Study : Year 2, Donaldsons Research Report, London.

LEE M and KENT E (1979) Caerphilly Hypermarket Study : Year 5, Donaldsons Research Report, London, 14.

LEE T R and WOOD L J (1980), "The city in an era of restricted car usage : some potential responses and adjustments to future oil shortages", Geoforum, 11, 17-29.

LEEMING F A (1959) "An experimental survey of retail shopping facilities in part of North Leeds", Transactions of the Institute of British Geographers, 26, 133-52.

LENTNEK B, LIEBER S R and SHESKIN I (1975) "Consumer behaviour in different areas", Annals of the Association of American Geographers, 65, 538-545.

LEONARD S (1979) "Managerialism, manager and self-management", Area, 11, 87-88.

LEONARD S (1982) "Urban managerialism : a period of transition", Progress in Human Geography, 190-215.

LIEBER S R (1977) "Attitudes and revealed behaviour: a case study", Professional Geographer, 29, 53-8.

LOJKINE J (1976) "Contribution to a Marxist theory of capitalist urbanization", in Pickvance C (Ed), Urban Socialism, London.

LOSCH A (1939) (1954) The Economics of Location (translated by Woglom W H and Stolper W F) Yale University Press, New Haven.

LYNCH K (1960) The Image of the City, Cambridge, Mass, MIT.

MADGE J (1953) The Tools of Social Science, Larman, London.

McEVOY D (1971) "Vacancy rates and the retail structure of the Manchester conurbation", paper given to IBG Urban Study Group meeting, Liverpool.

MACLARAN A (1981) "Area-based positive discrimination and the distribution of well-being", Transactions, Institute of British Geographers, 6, 53-67.

MACKAY D B (1976) "The effect of spatial stimuli on the estimation of cognitive maps", Geographical Analysis, 8, 439-52.

MACKAY D B, OLSHAVSKY R W and SENTELL G (1975) "Cognitive maps and spatial behavior of consumers", Geographical Analysis, 7, 19-34.

MACLENNAN D and WILLIAMS N J (1979) "Revealed space preference theory - a cautionary note", Tijdschrift voor Economische en Sociale Geografie, 70, 307-9.

McLOUGHLIN J B (1973) Control and Urban Planning, Faber and Faber, London.

MANCHESTER UNIVERSITY Dept of Town & Country Planning (1966)
Regional Shopping Centres : A Planning Report on N W England,
Parts 1 & 2, Manchester.

MARSH C (1982) The Survey Method : The Contribution of Survey
to Sociological Exploration, Allen & Unwin, London.

MATALAS N C and B J REIHER (1967) "Some comments on the use of
Factor Analysis", Water Resources Research, 3, 213-33.

MATHER P (1971) "Varimax and generality", Area, 3(4), 252-254.

MATHER P (1976) Computational Methods of Multivariate Analysis
in Physical Geography, London, Wiley.

MAXWELL A E (1961) "Recent trends in Factor Analysis", Journal
of the Royal Statistical Society, 124, 49-59.

MEGEE M (1964) "Factor analysis in hypothesis testing and
decision making", Professional Geographer, 16, 414-29.

MILLS E (1974) "Recent developments in retailing and urban
planning", Planning Research Applications Group, Topic
Paper, 3.

MINISTRY OF HOUSING AND LOCAL GOVERNMENT (1970) Development
Plans, HMSO, London.

MITCHELL C G B and TOWN S W (1977) "Accessibility of various
social groups to different activities", Transport and Road
Research Laboratory, Supplementary Report 258, Crowthorne,
Berks.

MOON G (1982) Political Geography and Public Services : A Case
Study of a Suburban Borough, unpublished PhD dissertation,
CNAA.

MOSELEY M (1979) Accessibility - The Rural Challenge, Methuen,
London.

MOSER C and KALTON E (1971) Survey Methods in Social Investigation, 2nd Ed., Heineman, London.

MOTTERSHAW B (1968) "Estimating shopping potential", Planning
Outlook, 5, 40-68.

MURDIE R (1965) "Cultural differences in consumer travel",
Economic Geography, 41, 211-33.

MURRAY D and SPENCER C (1979) "Individual differences in the
drawing of cognitive maps : the effects of geographical
mobility, strength of mental imagery and basic graphic
ability", Transactions of the Institute of British
Geographers, NS, 4, 385-91.

NACHMIAS D and NACHMIAS C (1976) Research Methods in the Social
Sciences, Edward Arnold, London.

NADER G A (1969) "Socio-economic status and consumer behaviour",
Urban Studies, 6, 235-45.

NEDO (1971) "The future pattern of shopping", National Economic
Development Office, London.

NEDO (1981) "Retailing in inner cities", National Economic
Development Office, Distributive Trades EDC, London.

NEDO (1985) "Employment Perspectives and the Distributive Trades", National Economic Development Office, London.
NELSON R L (1958) The Selection of Retail Locations, F W Dodge, New York.
NOAH (1973) in Harvey D (1973) Social Justice and the City.
NORMAN P (1975) "Managerialism : a review of recent work", Centre for Environmental Studies, cp 14, London.
O'BRIEN L G and GUY C M (1985) "A grocery price survey in Cardiff", UWIST Papers in Plan. Res., No. 84, Dept. of Town Planning, UWIST, Cardiff.
OFFICE OF POPULATION, Census and Surveys (1981), Census of Great Britain 1981.
OPENSHAW S (1973) "Insoluble problems in shopping model calibration when the trip pattern is not known", Regional Studies, 7, 367-71.
OPENSHAW S (1975) "Preference and perception: an analysis of consumer behaviour", Tijdschrift voor Economische en Sociale Geografie, 66, 84-92.
OPPENHEIM A N (1966) Questionnaire Design and Attitude Measurement, Heinemann, London.
OSGOOD G E, SUCI G J and TANNENBAUM P M (1957) The Measurement of Meaning, University of Illinois Press, Urbana.
OSGOOD G E (1959) "Semantic space revisited", Word, 15, 192-200.
OTTAR T (1974) "An introduction to Personal construct theory", Seminar paper, Environmental Psychology, University of Surrey.
PACIONE M (1975) "Preference and perception : an analysis of consumer behaviour", Tijdschrift voor Economische en Sociale Geografie, 66, 84-92.
PACIONE M (1979) "The in-town hypermarket : an innovation in the geography of retailing", Regional Studies, 13, 15-24.
PAHL R E (1965) "Trends in social geography", in Chorley R J and Haggett P (Eds) Frontiers in Geographical Teaching, Methuen, London, 81-100.
PAHL R E (1975) Whose City?, Penguin, Harmondsworth.
PAHL R E (1977) "Managers, technical experts and the state", in Harloe M (Ed) Captive Cities, Wiley, London, 49-60.
PAHL R E (1978) "Castells and collective consumption", Sociology, 12, 309-15.
PAHL R E (1979) "Socio-political factors in resource allocation", in Herbert D T and Smith D M (Eds) Social Problems and the City : Geographical Approaches, Oxford University Press, London, 33-46.
PALM R and PRED A (1976) "A time-geographic perspective of problems of inequality for women", in Burnett K P (Ed) A Social Geography of Women, Maarouffa, Chicago.
PARKER A J (1975) "Hypermarkets - the changing pattern of retailing", Geography, 60, 120-4.

PARKER A J (1976) Consumer Behaviour Motivation and Perception
: A Study of Dublin, Department of Geography, University
College, Dublin.
PATRICIOS N N (1979) "Human aspects of planning shopping
centers", Environment and Behaviour, 11, 511-38.
PATRICIOS N N (1980) "Relating-scale methodology for environ-
mental designs", Environment and Planning, B, 7, 273-87.
PENNY N and BROOM D (1986) "The Tesco approach to store
location", paper presented to ESRC Workshop, Bristol,
February.
PICKUP L (1981) "Housewives Mobility and Travel Patterns",
TRRL report No 97.
PINCH S P (1979) "Territorial justice in the city", in Herbert
D T and Smith D M (Eds) Social Problems and the City:
Geographical Perspectives, Oxford University Press, London,
201-223.
PIRIE G H (1976) "Thoughts on revealed preference and spatial
behaviour", Environment and Planning, 8A, 947-55.
PLANNER, The (1983) Planning`for Retail Change, 69(1).
PLANNING, TRANSPORTATION RESEARCH & COMPUTATION (1978)
Retailing Seminar, Summer annual conference seminar
proceedings, London.
PLANNING, TRANSPORTATION RESEARCH & COMPUTATION (1981)
Retailing Seminar, Summer annual conference seminar
proceedings, London.
POTTER R B (1976a) The Structural Characteristics of the Urban
Retailing System and the Nature of Consumer Behaviour and
Perception : A Case Study Based on Stockport, unpublished
PhD thesis, University of London.
POTTER R B (1976b) "Directional bias within the usage and
perceptual fields of urban consumers", Psychological Reports,
38, 988-90.
POTTER R B (1976c), "Spatial nature of consumer usage and
perceptual fields" Perceptual and Motor Skills, 43, 1185-86.
POTTER R B (1977a) "Spatial patterns of consumer behaviour and
perception in relation to the social class variable", Area,
9, 153-6.
POTTER R B (1977b) "Effects of age and family size on consumer
behaviour and perception", Perceptual and Motor Skills, 45,
842.
POTTER R B (1977c) "The nature of consumer usage fields in an
urban environment theoretical and empirical perspectives"
Tijdschrift voor Economische en Sociale Geografie, 68, 168-76.
POTTER R B (1978) "Aggregate consumer behaviour and perception
in relation to urban retailing structure: a preliminary
investigation", Tijdschrift voor Economische en Sociale
Geografie, 69, 345-52.

POTTER R B (1979a) "Perception of urban retailing facilities: an analysis of consumer information fields", Geografiska Annaler, 61B, 19-29.

POTTER R B (1979b) "Factors influencing consumer decision-making", Psychological Reports, 44, 674.

POTTER R B (1979c) "The morphological characteristics of urban retailing areas, a review and suggested methodology", Bedford College, University of London, Papers in Geography, 2.

POTTER R B (1980a) "Spatial and structural variations in the quality characteristics of intra-urban retailing centres", Transactions of the Institute of British Geographers, NS, 5, 207-28.

POTTER R B (1980b) "What is convenient shopping?", Town and Country Planning, 49, 115-17.

POTTER R B (1981a) "Correlates of urban retail area functional structure : an approach employing multivariate ordination", Professional Geographer, 33, 208-15.

POTTER R B (1981b) "The multivariate functional structure of the urban retailing system: a British case study", Transactions of the Institute of British Geographers, NS, 6, 188-213.

POTTER R B (1982) The Urban Retailing System, Gower, London.

QUIRK J and SAPOSNIK R (1968) Introduction to General Equilibrium Theory and Welfare Economics, New York.

RAY D M (1967) "Cultural differences in consumer travel behaviour in eastern Ontario", Canadian Geographer, 11, 143-56.

REILLY W J (1931) The Law of Retail Gravitation, Knickerbocker Press, New York.

RHODES T (1972), "Factors affecting the future location of new shopping developments in South Hampshire", South Hampshire Plan Technical Unit WP No 5.

RICH S U and JAIN S C (1968) "Social class and life cycle as predictors of shopping behaviour", J Market Research S, 41-49.

RIDGWAY J D (1976) "The future of district shopping centres - a retailer's view", Proceedings of the seminar on retailing, PTRC Summer Annual Meeting.

RIDGWAY J D (1981) "Modern retailing as a spur to urban regeneration", Proceedings, PTRC summer annual meeting and exhibition, Warwick, 19-28.

RIESER R L (1972) "Urban spatial images: an appraisal of the choice of respondents and measurement situation", London School of Economics, Graduate School of Geography Discussion Paper, No. 42.

ROGERS D S (1979) "Evaluating the business and planning impacts of suburban shopping centres", Regional Studies, 13(4), 395-408.

ROGERS D and GREEN H (1979) "A New perspective on forecasting store sales", The Geographical Review, LXIX, 449-468.

ROWEIS S T and SCOTT A F (1978) "The urban land question", in Cox K R (Ed) Urbanisation and Conflict in Market Societies, Maaroufa Press, Chicago, 38-73.

ROYCE J R (1958) "The development of factor analysis", Journal of General Psychology, 58, 139-64.

RUMMEL R J (1970) Applied Factor Analysis, Evanston, North-western University Press.

RUSHTON G (1969) "Analysis of spatial behaviour by revealed space preference", Annals of the Association of American Geographers, 59, 391-400.

RUSHTON G, GOLLEDGE R G and CLARK W A V (1967) "Formulation and test of a normative model for the spatial allocation of grocery expenditures by a dispersed population", Annals of the Association of American Geographers, 57, 389-400.

RUSHTON G (1971) "Postulates and properties of central place theory", Geographical Analysis, 3, 14-56.

RUSHTON G (1979) "Commentary on behavioral and perception geography", Annals of the Association of American Geography, 69, 463-4.

SAEY P and LAETNER M (1981) "On testing Christaller's theory : a rejoinder", Tidjschrift voor Economische en Sociale Geografie, 72(1), 50-51.

SANOFF H (1970) "House form and preference", in EDRA 2, 334-339.

SANOFF H and SAWHNEY M (1970) "Residential livability", in EDRA 2 proceedings, pp 13-8-1 to 13-8-10.

SARRE P (1972) "Perception", in Channels of Synthesis, Perception and Diffusion, Open University.

SAUNDERS P (1981) Social Theory and the Urban Question, Hutchinson, London.

SAUNDERS P (1982) "Towards a non spatial urban sociology", University of Sussex, Working Papers in Urban and Regional Studies.

SAUNDERS P (1983a), "Social theory and the urban question : a response to Prais and Kirby", Environment and Planning D, Society and Space 1, 234-239.

SAUNDERS P (1983b) Urban Politics, Hutchinson, London.

SCHILLER R K (1972) "The measurement of the attractiveness of shopping centres to middle class luxury consumers", Regional Studies, 6, 291-7.

SCHILLER R and LABER S (1977) "The quantity of major shopping development in Britain since 1965", Estates Gazette, 242, 359-363.

SCHILLER R (1979) "The responsibilities of retail planning", Chapter 1 in Davies R L (Ed) Retail Planning in the European Community, Saxon House, Farnborough.

SCHILLER R (1981a) "A model of retail branch distribution", Regional Studies, 15.

SCHILLER R (1981b) "Superstore impact", The Planner, 67, 38-40.

SCOTT P (1970) Geography and Retailing, Hutchinson, London.

SCOTTISH OFFICE (1981) The Elgin Fine Fare, Central Research Unit, Scottish Development Department.

SHAW G and WILLIAMS A (1980) "Structure plans and retail planning", Retail and Distribution Management, 8(1), 43-47.

SHAW G and WILLIAMS A (1982) "Structure plans and retail developments", Estates Gazette, 264, 25-27.

SHAW M (1980) "The analysis of a repertory grid", British Journal of Medical Psychology, 53, 117-126.

SHAW M and GAINES B R (1981) "Recent advances in the analysis of a repertory grid", British Journal of Medical Psychology, 54, 307-318.

SHEPHERD I D H and THOMAS C J (1980) "Urban consumer behaviour", Chapter 1 in Dawson J A (Ed) Retail Geography, Croom Helm.

SILK J (1982) "Comment on 'on the nature of explanation in human geography", Transactions of the Institute of British Geographers, 7, 3, 380-384.

SIMON H A (1957) Models of Man : Social and Rational, Wiley, New York.

SMART G (1977) "The future of structure plans", The Planner, Jan, 5-7.

SMITH (1964) in Harvey (1973) "Social justice and the City", p82, Edward Arnold, London.

SMITH D M (1977) Human Geography : A Welfare Approach, Edward Arnold, London.

SMITH D M (1979) "The identification of problems in cities : applications of social indicators", in Herbert D T and Smith D M (Eds), Social Problems and the City : Geographical Perspectives, Oxford University Press, Oxford, 13-32.

SPARKS L (1983) "Superstores and the inner city - some reflections", Retail and Distribution Management, Jan/Feb.

SPENCER A H (1978), "Deriving measures of attractiveness for shopping centres", Regional Studies, 12, 713-26.

SPENCER A H (1979) Customer Behaviour and Perception of Shopping Centres, unpublished PhD thesis, University of Reading.

SPENCER A H (1980) "Cognition and shopping choice : a multidimensional scaling approach", Environment and Planning, A, 12, 1235-51.

STEA D (1973) "Rats, men and spatial behavior, all revisited", Professional Geographer, 25, 196-112.

STONE G (1954) "City shoppers and urban identification: observations on the social psychology of city life", American Journal of Sociology, 60, 35-54.

STRACHAN A (1971) "Car parks and shopping", Estates Gazette, 220, 199.

STRINGER P (1972) "Psychological significance in personal and supplied construct systems", European Journal of Social Psychology, 2, 437-447.

STRINGER P and TERRY P (1978) "Objective constructs and cognitive structure", British Journal of Medical Psychology, US1, 325-335.

TAEUBER K E and TAEUBER A F (1965) Negroes in Cities : Residential Segregation and Neighbourhood Change, Aldine, Chicago.

TEITZ M B (1968) "Towards a theory of urban public facility location", Papers and Proceedings of the Regional Science Association, 21, 35-51.

THOMAS C J (1974) "The effects of social class and car ownership on intraurban shopping behaviour in Greater Swansea", Cambria, 2, 98-126.

THOMAS C J (1976) "Sociospatial differentiation and the use of services", in Herbert D T and Johnston R J (Eds), Social Areas in Cities, Vol 2, Ch.1, John Wiley, London, 17-63.

THOMAS C J (1978) Retail Change in South Wales, Retail Planning Associates, Corbridge, England.

THOMAS M (1976) "Planners outdistanced by retailers' speed of change", Built Environment, 2(3), 194-9.

THORPE D (1974) Research into Retailing and Distribution, Saxon House, Farnborough, Hants.

THORPE D (1975a) "Assessing the need for shops : or can planners plan?" Proceedings of the seminar on retailing, PTRC Summer Annual Meeting.

THORPE D (1975b) "Retail planning : the key policy issues", paper given at symposium: Town Planning for Retailing, Retail Outlets Research Unit, Manchester Business School.

THORPE D, SHEPHERD P M and BATES P (1976) "Food retailers and superstore competition : a study of short term impact in York, Northampton and Cambridge", Retail Outlets Research Unit, Manchester Business School, Research Report, 25.

THORPE D (1977a) "Shopping trip patterns and the spread of superstores and hypermarkets in Great Britain", Manchester Business School, Retail Outlets Research Unit, Research Paper, 10.

THORPE D (1977b) "Superstores, shopping trips and public policy in Great Britain" in Williams A F (Ed), Transport and Public Policy, IBG Transport Group, London.

THORPE D and McGOLDRICK P J (1974) "Carrefour, Caerphilly : consumer reaction", Manchester Business School, Retail Outlets Research Unit, Research Report, 12.

TIMMERMANS H (1979) "A spatial preference model of regional shopping behaviour", Tijdschrift voor Economische en Sociale Geografie, 70, 45-8.

TIMMERMANS H (1980a) "Undimensional conjoint measurement models and consumer decision-making", Area, 12, 291-300.

TIMMERMANS H (1980b) "Consumer spatial choice strategies: a comparative study of some alternative behavioural spatial shopping models", Geoforum, 11, 123-31.

TIMMERMANS H (1981a), "Spatial choice behaviour in different environmental settings : an application of the revealed preference approach", Geografiska Annaler, 63B, 57-67.

TIMMERMANS H (1981b) "Multi-attribute shopping models and ridge regression analysis", Environment and Planning A, 13, 43-56.

TIMMERMANS H and RUSHTON G (1979) "Revealed space preference theory - a rejoinder", Tijdschrift voor Economische en Sociale Geografie, 70, 309-12.

TIMMERMANS H, VAN DER HEIJDEN R and WESTERVELD H (1981) "Perception of urban retailing environments : an empirical analysis of consumer information usage fields", University of Technology, Eindhoven, Department of Architecture, Building and Planning Working Paper.

TIMMERMANS H et al (1982a) "Cognition of urban retailing structures: a Dutch case study", Tijdschrift voor Economische en Sociale Geografie, 73(1), 2-12.

TIMMERMANS H et al (1982b) "Perception of urban retailing environments", Geoforum, 13.

TIVERS J (1977) Constraints on Spatial Activity Patterns : Women With Young Children, King's College, London, Department of Geography, Occasional Paper, 6.

TOWN S W (1980) "The social distribution of mobility and travel patterns", TRRL Report, No 948, Crowthorne, Berks.

TOWNSEND P and DAVIDSON N (1982) Inequalities in Health, Harmondsworth.

TUAN Y F (1975) "Images and mental maps", Annals of the Association of American Geographers, 65, 205-13.

TUAN Y F (1976) "Humanistic geography", Annals of the Association of American Geographers, 66, 266-76.

TURNER R and COLE H (1980) "An investigation into the estimation and reliability of urban shopping models", Urban Studies, 17, 139-57.

URPI (1977) District Shopping Centres, Report of an URPI Workshop, The Unit for Retail Planning Information Limited, Reading.

WADE B (1979) "Retail planning in Britain", Chapter 3 in Davies, R L (Ed) Retail Planning in the European Community, Saxon House, 51-63.

WALTERS D (1974) "Retail site location, time for a new approach?", Retail and Distribution Management, 2(6), 28-31.

WARNES A M and DANIELS P W (1978) "Intra-urban shopping travel : a review of theory and evidence from British towns", paper presented to the Annual Conference of the Institute of British Geographers.

WARNES A M and DANIELS P W (1980) "Urban retail distributions:
an appraisal of the empirical foundations of retail geography",
Geoforum, 11, 133-46.
WARREN N (1966) "Social class and construct systems", British
Journal of Social and Clinical Psychology, 5, 254-63.
WEBBER M M (1963) "Order in diversity : community without
propinquity", in Wingo L (Jr) (Ed) Cities and Space, The
Future Use of Urban Land, Johns Hopkins Press, Baltimore,
23-54.
WEINRICH J (1958) "Travel through semantic space", Word, 14,
346-66.
WILKINSON J H (1965) The Algebraic Eigenvalue Problem, Oxford,
Clarendon Press.
WILLIAMS J and ARNOTT C (1977) "A new look at retail forecasts",
The Planner, 63(6), 170-172.
WILLIAMS P (1978) "Urban managerialism : a concept of
relevance?", Area, 10, 236-240.
WILLIAMS N J (1979) "The definition of shopper types as an aid
in the anaylsis of spatial consumer behaviour", Tijdschrift
voor Economische en Sociale Geografie, 70, 157-63.
WILLIAMS N J (1981) "Attitudes and consumer spatial behaviour",
Tijdschrift voor Economische en Sociale Geografie, 72, 145-54.
WILSON A G (1974) Urban and Regional Models in Geography and
Planning, Wiley, London.
WILSON A G (1976b) "Retailers profits and consumer's welfare
in spatial interaction shopping Models" in Masser I (Ed)
Theory and Practise in Regional Science, Pion, London, 42-59.
WILSON A G (1981) Geography and the Environment : Systems
Analytical Methods", John Wiley, Chichester.
WOOD L J and LEE T R (1980) "Time-space convergence :
reappraisal for an oil short future", Area, 12, 217-22.
WRIGLEY N (1980) "An approach to the modelling of shop-choice
patterns : an explanatory analysis of purchasing patterns in
a British city", in Herbert D T and Johnston R J (Eds)
Geography and the Urban Environment, Wiley, London.
WRIGLEY N, GUY C M, DUNN R and O'BRIEN L G (1985) "The Cardiff
consumer panel, methodological aspects of a long-term panel
survey", Transactions of the Institute of British Geographers,
NS, 10, 63-76.
YEATES M and GARNER B J (1980/1971) The North American City,
(Third/First Editions), Harper and Row, New York.
ZWEIG F (1948) Labour, Life and Poverty, London.